KAUAI TRAVEL GUIDE 2024 EDITION

TABLE OF CONTENT

SECTION 6: SHOPPING

- *Local Markets*

- *Souvenirs*

- *Unique Finds*

SECTION 7: CULTURE AND HISTORY

- *Native Hawaiian Culture*

- *Historical Sites*

- *Museums and Exhibits*

- *Annual Events*

INTRODUCTION

Welcome to Kauai

Welcome to Kauai, a paradise nestled in the heart of the Pacific Ocean. This emerald jewel, part of the Hawaiian archipelago, captivates visitors with its lush landscapes, pristine beaches, and vibrant culture. As you step onto the Garden Isle, you are greeted by a symphony of colors, sounds, and scents that define the essence of Kauai.

Kauai, often referred to as the "Garden Isle," is the oldest and fourth-largest island in the Hawaiian chain. Its age has bestowed upon it a unique topography characterized by jagged cliffs, deep valleys, and a dramatic coastline. The island's diverse ecosystems, ranging from rainforests to arid plains, create a mosaic of natural wonders that beckon exploration.

The warm embrace of the tropical sun welcomes you as you set foot on Kauai's shores. With an average annual temperature ranging from 70 to 85 degrees Fahrenheit (21-29°C), the climate is a perfect companion for your island adventures. Whether you're seeking relaxation or thrill-seeking escapades, Kauai offers a tapestry of experiences that cater to every taste.

One cannot escape the allure of Kauai's iconic landmarks. The Na Pali Coast, a rugged masterpiece of towering cliffs and lush valleys, stands as a testament to the island's geological marvels. The breathtaking views from Kalalau Lookout will etch themselves into your memory, inviting you to marvel at the raw, untamed beauty of nature.

Waimea Canyon, often hailed as the "Grand Canyon of the Pacific," is a kaleidoscope of colors that stretches over 14 miles long and reaches depths of 3,600 feet. The canyon's red and green hues, formed by centuries of erosion, create a mesmerizing spectacle that lures photographers, hikers, and nature enthusiasts alike.

Hanalei Bay, nestled on Kauai's north shore, is a serene crescent of golden sand bordered by emerald mountains. The quaint town of Hanalei exudes a laid-back charm, inviting you to immerse yourself in the local culture. Explore the vibrant art scene, indulge in farm-to-table dining, or simply stroll along the historic Hanalei Pier as the sun dips below the horizon.

The allure of Poipu Beach, on the sunny south shore, lies in its powdery sand and turquoise waters. Snorkel alongside colorful marine life, bask in the sun, or try your hand at surfing.

Poipu's diverse marine ecosystem, including the resident Hawaiian monk seals, provides a unique opportunity to connect with the island's rich biodiversity.

Wailua River, flowing through the heart of Kauai, is a sacred waterway intertwined with Hawaiian folklore. Embark on a boat tour to the Fern Grotto, a natural amphitheater adorned with hanging ferns, and feel the mana (spiritual energy) that emanates from this mystical place.

Kauai's activities extend far beyond its stunning landscapes. Hiking enthusiasts can traverse the famous Kalalau Trail along the Na Pali Coast or embark on the challenging Awa'awapuhi Trail for panoramic views of the island's interior. Adventure seekers can take to the skies on a helicopter tour, witnessing hidden waterfalls and inaccessible landscapes that showcase Kauai's untamed beauty.

Immerse yourself in the island's cultural tapestry through authentic experiences. Engage in a traditional Hawaiian luau, where the rhythm of hula and the taste of poi connect you to the roots of Polynesian heritage. Visit local markets to savor the flavors of fresh pineapple, coconut, and poke, or attend cultural festivals that celebrate the island's diverse heritage.

Accommodations on Kauai range from luxury resorts overlooking the ocean to cozy beachfront cottages. Whether you choose to unwind in a spa resort or opt for a more rustic camping experience, Kauai offers a range of options to suit every traveler's preference and budget.

The island's dining scene is a gastronomic journey, with a fusion of flavors influenced by its multicultural history. From traditional Hawaiian dishes to international cuisine, Kauai's restaurants, food trucks, and farmers' markets ensure a culinary adventure that mirrors the island's diversity.

As you traverse Kauai's scenic byways, you'll discover charming towns where local artisans showcase their craft. From handmade jewelry to traditional crafts, these treasures serve as tangible reminders of your journey through Kauai.

Venture into the island's rich history by exploring ancient heiaus (temples) and petroglyphs. Learn about the Hawaiian monarchy at historical sites like the Kilohana Estate, where a glimpse into the past reveals the intricate stories that shape Kauai's cultural narrative.

Practical considerations, such as weather patterns and local customs, enhance your understanding of this enchanting island. Kauai's residents, known for their warm hospitality, welcome you with the spirit of aloha, creating an atmosphere where every visitor feels like a cherished guest.

Throughout the year, Kauai hosts a variety of events and festivals that showcase its vibrant culture. From the lively Waimea Town Celebration to the cultural immersion of the Kauai Polynesian Festival, these gatherings provide an opportunity to connect with the local community and celebrate the island's traditions.

Island day trips offer a chance to explore neighboring isles and expand your Hawaiian experience. Whether it's a short boat ride to Niihau, the "Forbidden Isle," or a flight to Oahu to witness the dynamic energy of Honolulu, Kauai serves as a gateway to the broader wonders of Hawaii.

Wildlife and nature enthusiasts will find solace in Kauai's rich biodiversity. The island is a haven for birdwatchers, with the elusive nene (Hawaiian goose) and vibrant native birds gracing the skies. Marine life flourishes in the crystal-clear waters, providing snorkelers and divers with a front-row seat to the underwater spectacle.

For those seeking relaxation and rejuvenation, Kauai offers a range of health and wellness activities. Indulge in spa treatments inspired by ancient Hawaiian practices, practice yoga amidst lush surroundings, or engage in outdoor fitness activities that harmonize with the island's natural beauty.

As you delve into Kauai's communities, you'll discover the essence of local life. Interviews with residents provide insights into the island's sustainable initiatives and the delicate balance between preserving Kauai's natural splendor and welcoming visitors.

In the appendix, detailed maps assist you in navigating the island's diverse landscapes. Useful contacts ensure you have access to essential services, and a glossary provides a deeper understanding of the unique terminology woven into Kauai's cultural fabric.

Welcome to Kauai, where every sunrise paints a new chapter in this Pacific paradise. Whether you seek adventure, cultural enrichment, or tranquility, Kauai invites you to embark on a journey where the spirit of aloha is not just a greeting but a way of life.

Overview of Kauai

Kauai, often referred to as the "Garden Isle," is a captivating and lush island situated in the central Pacific. It is the oldest of the main Hawaiian Islands, boasting a unique blend of natural beauty, rich cultural heritage, and a laid-back atmosphere. Spanning approximately 552 square miles, Kauai is the fourth-largest island in the archipelago, and its diverse landscapes make it a haven for outdoor enthusiasts and those seeking a tranquil escape.

The island's geography is nothing short of spectacular. From the rugged cliffs of the Na Pali Coast to the awe-inspiring Waimea Canyon, often dubbed the "Grand Canyon of the Pacific," Kauai's topography is a testament to the forces of nature. The Na Pali Coast, with its emerald

reen cliffs and deep blue waters, remains one of the most iconic and photogenic coastlines
lobally, drawing hikers, boaters, and nature lovers from around the world.

Waimea Canyon, located in the western part of the island, is a geological marvel with its vibrant
ed and orange hues. The canyon, carved by the Waimea River over millions of years, offers
breathtaking panoramic views and numerous hiking trails for those eager to explore its depths.

auai's natural wonders extend beyond these famous landmarks, encompassing lush
ainforests, cascading waterfalls, and serene beaches.

he Island's climate varies across its microclimates, creating distinct environments. The north
hore, for instance, is known for its tropical rainforests and receives more rainfall, while the
outh shore tends to be sunnier and drier. This diversity contributes to Kauai's vibrant
cosystems, supporting a wide array of flora and fauna. Visitors can witness this biodiversity in
laces like the Limahuli Garden and Preserve, a botanical garden dedicated to preserving native
Hawaiian plants.

Kauai's cultural heritage is deeply rooted in the traditions of the native Hawaiian people. The
sland is home to historical sites, such as the ancient Menehune Fishpond, believed to be built
y the Menehune, a mythical race of people. The Wailua Complex of Heiaus, a series of ancient
emples and ceremonial sites, provides a glimpse into the island's spiritual past.

he fusion of Hawaiian culture with influences from other cultures, including European and
Asian, is evident in Kauai's cuisine, arts, and traditions. Local markets and festivals showcase
he island's commitment to preserving and celebrating its diverse heritage. Visitors can savor
raditional Hawaiian dishes, often featuring fresh, locally sourced ingredients, and immerse
hemselves in the sounds of traditional Hawaiian music and dance.

Kauai's charm extends beyond its natural and cultural offerings to the warmth and hospitality
f its residents. The island's communities embrace a slower pace of life, emphasizing the
mportance of balance and connection to the land. This attitude contributes to a sense of
ranquility that envelops visitors, making Kauai a sought-after destination for those seeking
oth adventure and relaxation.

As a destination, Kauai offers a myriad of activities for every type of traveler. Whether it's
xploring the underwater world through snorkeling, embarking on a scenic helicopter tour, or
imply unwinding on one of the pristine beaches, the options are as diverse as the island itself.
he laid-back atmosphere and breathtaking landscapes create an idyllic setting for romantic
etaways, family vacations, and outdoor adventures.

n essence, Kauai is a masterpiece of nature, a canvas painted with lush greenery, dramatic
oastlines, and vibrant culture. Its allure lies not only in its physical beauty but in the spirit of
loha that permeates every corner of the island. Kauai invites visitors to disconnect from the

hustle and bustle of the modern world and reconnect with the essence of life, surrounded by the beauty of the Pacific and the embrace of the Garden Isle.

Why Visit Kauai in 2024

Kauai, often referred to as the "Garden Isle," is a paradisiacal gem in the Pacific Ocean that beckons travelers with its lush landscapes, pristine beaches, and vibrant culture. As 2024 unfolds, there are compelling reasons why Kauai should be at the top of your travel list. From breathtaking natural wonders to cultural experiences that leave a lasting imprint, Kauai offers an enchanting escape for every type of adventurer.

The allure of Kauai lies In its unparalleled natural beauty. The Na Pali Coast, with its towering emerald cliffs and cascading waterfalls, is a testament to the island's dramatic and unspoiled scenery. As you traverse the coastline, either by hiking the challenging Kalalau Trail or embarking on a boat tour, you'll be awe-struck by the sheer magnificence of nature. In 2024, these vistas remain as pristine as ever, providing a timeless escape from the hustle and bustle of everyday life.

Waimea Canyon, often dubbed the "Grand Canyon of the Pacific," is another testament to Kauai's geological wonders. The canyon's vibrant red and green hues create a striking contrast, making it a must-visit for photographers and nature enthusiasts alike. The panoramic views from the canyon's lookout points offer a captivating glimpse into the island's geological history, providing a deeper understanding of Kauai's natural evolution.

For those seeking tranquility, Hanalei Bay is a haven of serenity. This crescent-shaped bay, surrounded by lush mountains, is a postcard-perfect destination. Whether you're lazing on the beach, trying your hand at surfing, or exploring the charming town of Hanalei, the bay encapsulates the laid-back spirit that defines Kauai. In 2024, the timeless appeal of Hanalei Bay remains undiminished, making it an idyllic retreat for those in search of peace and relaxation.

Kauai's diverse range of activities caters to every adventurer's desire. Hiking enthusiasts can explore the island's extensive network of trails, from the challenging Kalalau Trail to the more accessible Waimea Canyon trails. Water lovers can partake in snorkeling adventures in crystal-clear waters, discovering the vibrant marine life that thrives beneath the surface. Thrill-seekers can experience the exhilaration of zip-lining through the lush canopy or take to the skies on a helicopter tour for a bird's-eye view of Kauai's wonders.

Beyond its natural splendors, Kauai invites visitors to immerse themselves in its rich cultural tapestry. Native Hawaiian culture is celebrated throughout the island, from traditional hula erformances to the artistry of local craftsmen. Exploring ancient sites such as the Wailua River nd its sacred Fern Grotto provides insight into the island's historical and spiritual significance. 2024, Kauai continues to be a living canvas where the past and present converge, offering a nique cultural experience for every visitor.

ccommodations on the island cater to a variety of preferences, ensuring that your stay is as omfortable as it is memorable. Whether you choose a luxurious resort with oceanfront views, cozy boutique hotel nestled in the heart of a charming town, or a rustic cabin surrounded by ature, Kauai offers a range of options to suit your style.

ulinary enthusiasts will find Kauai's dining scene to be a delectable journey into local flavors. resh, farm-to-table ingredients form the basis of the island's cuisine, with an emphasis on eafood and tropical fruits. From casual beachside eateries to upscale restaurants, Kauai's iverse culinary landscape reflects the island's fusion of cultures and commitment to ustainability.

hopping on the island is a unique experience, with local markets offering handmade crafts, ewelry, and artisanal goods. Supporting local businesses not only allows you to take home a iece of Kauai's charm but also contributes to the island's vibrant community.

s you plan your visit to Kauai in 2024, consider the practicalities that enhance your experience. he island's weather, while generally mild, can vary, so packing accordingly ensures you're repared for any adventure. Safety tips, including respecting the environment and local ustoms, contribute to a harmonious and enjoyable stay.

auai's calendar is dotted with events and festivals that showcase the island's spirit and raditions. Whether you find yourself joining in on a local celebration or witnessing a traditional eremony, these experiences create lasting memories and deepen your connection to the sland.

conclusion, Kauai's timeless allure, coupled with the freshness of a new year, makes it an deal destination in 2024. Whether you seek adventure, relaxation, cultural exploration, or a bit f everything, Kauai welcomes you with open arms. As you embark on this journey to the arden Isle, prepare to be captivated by the magic of Kauai—a destination that transcends time nd leaves an indelible mark on your soul.

SECTION 1: GETTING STARTED

The Best Time to Visit Kauai: A Comprehensive Guide

Kauai, often referred to as the "Garden Isle," is a stunning tropical paradise that attracts visitor year-round. While the island boasts pleasant weather throughout the year, there are certain times when it shines brightest, offering an ideal combination of climate, activities, and natural beauty. In this guide, we'll delve into the nuances of the best time to visit Kauai, considering factors such as weather patterns, crowd levels, and special events that can enhance your overall experience.

Kauai enjoys a tropical climate, characterized by warm temperatures and consistent trade winds. The island experiences two main seasons: the dry season (Kau) and the wet season (Ho'oilo). These seasons, however, can vary across different regions of the island.

Dry Season (April to October):

The dry season is the most popular time to visit Kauai, attracting a large number of tourists seeking sun-soaked days and clear skies. During these months, temperatures range from the mid-70s to the high 80s Fahrenheit (24-32°C). The weather is generally more predictable, making it an excellent time for outdoor activities such as hiking, snorkeling, and beach outings.

One of the highlights of the dry season is the calmer ocean conditions, creating ideal circumstances for water-based activities. Whether you're exploring the vibrant coral reefs or embarking on a boat tour along the majestic Na Pali Coast, the dry season provides optimal conditions for aquatic adventures.

Wet Season (November to March):

The wet season is characterized by occasional rain showers and a slightly higher chance of overcast skies. While rainfall is more prevalent during these months, it's essential to understand that Kauai's microclimates mean that the weather can vary significantly from one area to another. The North Shore tends to receive more rainfall than the South and West sides

Despite the increased chance of rain, the wet season has its advantages. The island is lush and green during this time, showcasing Kauai's natural beauty at its peak. Waterfalls cascade down he verdant cliffs, and the landscapes are a tapestry of vibrant hues. For travelers who don't mind occasional rain showers, the wet season offers a unique and breathtaking experience.

Another crucial factor to consider when planning your visit to Kauai is the level of tourist activity on the island. The peak tourist season aligns with the dry season, particularly during school holidays and major U.S. holidays. If you prefer a more tranquil experience and lower accommodation costs, consider visiting during the shoulder seasons—spring and fall—when the weather is still favorable, and crowds are more manageable.

Kauai hosts various events and festivals throughout the year, providing an added layer of excitement for visitors. From cultural celebrations to food and music festivals, these events offer a chance to immerse yourself in the local scene. Check the calendar to see if your visit coincides with any of these festivities, enhancing your overall experience and giving you a deeper understanding of Kauai's rich cultural tapestry.

The best time to visit Kauai depends on your preferences and priorities. Whether you're seeking sun-drenched days for outdoor activities or you're captivated by the lush, green landscapes of the wet season, Kauai has something to offer year-round. Consider the climate, crowd levels, and special events that align with your interests, and plan your visit accordingly. Regardless of when you choose to visit, the Garden Isle is sure to leave you with unforgettable memories of its beauty and hospitality.

Travel Tips and Etiquette

Traveling to Kauai is an exciting adventure that promises stunning landscapes, vibrant culture, and unforgettable experiences. To ensure a smooth and enjoyable journey, it's essential to be mindful of travel tips and etiquette. Whether you're a first-time visitor or a seasoned traveler, these insights will help you navigate the island with respect and cultural sensitivity.

1. Respect the 'Aina (Land):

Kauai's natural beauty is awe-inspiring, and it's crucial to treat the island with the utmost respect. Stay on designated trails when hiking, avoid disturbing wildlife, and adhere to any posted guidelines. Responsible tourism helps preserve Kauai's unique ecosystem for generations to come.

2. Embrace the 'Aloha Spirit':

The Aloha Spirit is more than just a phrase; it's a way of life in Hawaii. Embrace the warmth, friendliness, and openness that locals exhibit. Greet people with a genuine "aloha," and you'll find that the island's inhabitants are more than happy to share their culture and recommendations.

3. Sustainable Practices:

Kauai is committed to sustainability, and visitors are encouraged to adopt eco-friendly practices. Reduce your environmental impact by using reusable water bottles, minimizing plastic usage, and participating in beach clean-up initiatives. By treading lightly, you contribute to the preservation of Kauai's natural wonders.

4. Dress Appropriately:

Kauai's climate is generally warm, but it's essential to dress modestly when visiting cultural or religious sites. Swimwear is appropriate at the beach, but cover up when exploring other areas. Additionally, pack comfortable shoes for exploring the island's diverse terrain.

5. Learn Some Hawaiian Phrases:

While English is widely spoken, learning a few basic Hawaiian phrases demonstrates respect for the local culture. Mahalo (thank you) and aloha (hello/goodbye) go a long way in connecting with the community.

6. Understand Laid-Back Time:

The pace of life in Kauai is relaxed, and locals operate on "island time." Embrace this laid-back attitude and be patient, especially in service-related situations. Enjoy the opportunity to slow down and savor the moment.

7. Bring Cash:

While credit cards are widely accepted, having some cash on hand is practical, especially in more remote areas. It ensures you can make purchases from local vendors and participate in cash-only activities.

8. Follow Trail Etiquette:

auai boasts an extensive network of hiking trails, each offering breathtaking views. Follow trail tiquette by yielding to oncoming hikers, staying on marked paths, and respecting any posted ules. This ensures a positive experience for both you and fellow adventurers.

9. Be Mindful of Wildlife:

auai is home to diverse wildlife, including endangered species. Keep a safe distance from nimals, especially monk seals and sea turtles. Admire them from afar, and avoid disturbing heir natural behavior.

10. Participate in Cultural Events:

your visit coincides with local festivals or events, consider participating to gain deeper insights to Hawaiian culture. Festivals often feature traditional music, dance, and cuisine, providing a ich cultural experience.

y incorporating these travel tips and etiquette into your journey, you not only enhance your wn experience but also contribute to the preservation of Kauai's natural and cultural heritage. raveling with respect and mindfulness ensures a harmonious and fulfilling adventure on this nchanting island.

SECTION 2: EXPLORING THE BEAUTY OF KAUAI: TOP ATTRACTIONS AND THEIR ADDRESSES

Kauai, the Garden Isle of Hawaii, is a paradise of natural wonders, vibrant culture, and breathtaking landscapes. Whether you're an adventure seeker, a nature lover, or someone seeking tranquility, Kauai has something to offer for everyone. Here are some of the top attractions, each accompanied by its address for your convenience.

1. Na Pali Coast State Wilderness Park

Address: End of Hwy 560, Haena, HI 96714

The iconic Na Pali Coast is a must-see for any visitor to Kauai. Towering emerald cliffs, lush valleys, and cascading waterfalls create a mesmerizing backdrop. Accessible by hiking, boat tours, or helicopter rides, the Na Pali Coast promises an unforgettable experience.

2. Waimea Canyon State Park

Address: Waimea Canyon Dr, Waimea, HI 96796

Known as the "Grand Canyon of the Pacific," Waimea Canyon is a geological marvel with its red and green-hued canyon walls. Scenic lookouts offer panoramic views, and adventurous visitor can explore hiking trails for a closer encounter with this natural wonder.

3. Hanalei Bay

Address: Hanalei, HI 96714

Nestled on Kauai's north shore, Hanalei Bay is a postcard-perfect beach with a charming small town. Enjoy water activities, relax on the golden sands, and take in the view of verdant mountains. Hanalei Bay is not just a beach; it's a destination that captures the heart.

4. Poipu Beach Park

Address: Hoona Rd, Koloa, HI 96756

For sun-seekers and water enthusiasts, Poipu Beach is a haven. This south shore gem offers crystal-clear waters, ideal for snorkeling and swimming. The adjacent park provides picnic areas, making it a perfect spot for a day of fun and relaxation.

5. Wailua River State Park

Address: Hwy 56 & 580, Lihue, HI 96766

Explore the Wailua River, Hawaii's only navigable river, with a boat tour or kayak adventure. The park also hosts the Wailua Falls, a stunning double-tiered waterfall accessible by a short hike. Immerse yourself in the beauty of the lush surroundings.

These are just a glimpse of the enchanting attractions that await you in Kauai. Each corner of the island has its unique charm and beauty, inviting you to discover the wonders of this tropical paradise.

Na Pali Coast State Wilderness Park

Nestled on the northwest side of Kauai, the Na Pali Coast State Wilderness Park stands as a testament to the raw, unbridled beauty of the Hawaiian islands. This pristine stretch of coastline, often hailed as one of the most breathtaking in the world, is a haven for adventurers, nature enthusiasts, and those seeking solace in the embrace of untouched landscapes.

At the heart of Na Pali's allure is its rugged, emerald cliffs that dramatically rise from the cerulean waters of the Pacific. These cliffs, sculpted by centuries of wind and waves, create a mesmerizing panorama that has captivated artists, writers, and travelers throughout history. The sheer magnitude of the cliffs, some reaching heights of over 4,000 feet, imparts a sense of awe and reverence as you stand in their shadow.

The journey to Na Pali Is as much a part of the experience as the destination itself. Accessible primarily by boat, helicopter, or on foot, each mode of transportation offers a unique perspective on the unfolding beauty. Boat tours, departing from the nearby town of Hanalei or Port Allen, take visitors along the coast, revealing hidden sea caves, pristine beaches, and the occasional playful dolphin escort.

For those seeking an aerial view, helicopter tours provide a breathtaking panorama of Na Pali's undulating cliffs and lush valleys. The choppers weave through the valleys, offering a bird's-eye view of waterfalls cascading down the rugged terrain, creating ephemeral silver threads against the vibrant green backdrop.

For the intrepid hiker, the Kalalau Trail presents an opportunity to immerse oneself fully in the untamed splendor of Na Pali. The trail, stretching 11 miles one way, weaves along the coast and through verdant valleys, providing a challenging yet immensely rewarding experience for those willing to navigate its twists and turns. Hiking the Kalalau Trail is a pilgrimage through time, as you traverse ancient Hawaiian settlements, witness sacred sites, and encounter the diverse flora and fauna that call this rugged coastline home.

One of the trail's highlights is Hanakapi'ai Beach, a pristine stretch of golden sand nestled between towering cliffs and the restless sea. The beach serves as a resting point for hikers and a destination in itself for those seeking a day of sun and surf. The brave can venture further to Hanakapi'ai Falls, an ethereal cascade surrounded by lush vegetation, offering a refreshing reprieve for the weary traveler.

As you navigate the Kalalau Trail, the sheer isolation of Na Pali becomes apparent. The untouched wilderness, the absence of roads, and the limited access contribute to a sense of remoteness that transports visitors to a different era. It's a place where the modern world fades away, leaving only the sound of the wind, the crashing waves, and the chorus of birds echoing through the valleys.

The cultural significance of Na Pal" adds another layer to its allure. The ancient Hawaiians, deeply connected to the land and sea, revered this coastline as a sacred place. The remnants of their presence, including heiau (temples) and ancient terraced agricultural sites, offer a glimpse into the rich history of the indigenous people who once thrived in harmony with this challenging yet rewarding environment.

Na Pali is not merely a destination; it's an immersive journey into the heart of nature's grandeur. The rugged cliffs, the vibrant marine life, and the lush valleys each contribute to a narrative of resilience and beauty. As the sun sets over the Pacific, casting a warm glow on the cliffs and turning the sea into a palette of oranges and pinks, Na Pali reveals itself as a sanctuary for those seeking solace, adventure, and a profound connection to the natural world.

The Na Pali Coast State Wilderness Park is a testament to the unparalleled beauty of Kauai. Whether witnessed from the deck of a boat, the window of a helicopter, or the soles of a hiker's boots, Na Pali leaves an indelible impression, inviting all who encounter it to appreciate the delicate balance between the raw power of nature and the enduring spirit of those who call this enchanting island home.

Waimea Canyon State Park: A Majestic Tapestry of Nature's Grandeur

auai, Waimea Canyon State Park stands as a testament to the awe-inspiring beauty of nature.)ften referred to as the "Grand Canyon of the Pacific," this geological wonder is a masterpiece f rugged terrain, vibrant colors, and unparalleled vistas that leave visitors breathless. Spanning ver 14 miles in length, one mile in width, and reaching depths of up to 3,600 feet, Waimea anyon is a mesmerizing destination that beckons adventurers, hikers, and nature enthusiasts like.

Vaimea Canyon is a geological marvel, carved over millions of years by the erosive forces of vind and water. The result is a breathtaking landscape featuring deep gorges, towering cliffs, nd layered canyon walls that showcase a spectrum of colors. The canyon's palette transitions rom earthy reds and oranges to lush greens, creating a vivid tapestry that changes with the ngle of the sun. It's a living canvas that tells the story of Kauai's geological history, captivating ll who gaze upon it.

journey to Waimea Canyon is a journey into the heart of Kauai's interior. Scenic lookouts dot he canyon's rim, providing visitors with unparalleled views of the vast expanse below. The nost famous of these viewpoints is the Waimea Canyon Lookout, easily accessible by car. From his vantage point, visitors are treated to a panoramic spectacle of the canyon, with the winding Vaimea River carving its way through the rugged terrain.

urther along the canyon rim, the Pu'u Hinahina Lookout offers a different perspective, howcasing the canyon's layered cliffs and the distant Pacific Ocean. As the sunlight dances pon the canyon walls, the colors shift, revealing the intricate details of the geological ormations. These lookouts serve as windows into the heart of Waimea Canyon, inviting ontemplation and reflection.

or those seeking a more intimate encounter with Waimea Canyon, a network of hiking trails risscross the park, leading adventurers into its depths. The Canyon Trail, also known as the ukui Trail, descends into the canyon, offering hikers a closer look at the geological features nd diverse flora. The challenge of the descent is rewarded with stunning views of Waimea iver and the canyon walls.

or a more extended trek, the Waimea Canyon Trail connects with the Alakai Swamp Trail, eading hikers to the summit of Waialeale, one of the wettest spots on Earth. Along the way, he landscape transforms from the arid canyon floor to the mist-shrouded realms of the Alakai wamp, providing a unique and diverse hiking experience.

Waimea Canyon is not only a geological wonder but also a haven for diverse plant and animal life. The canyon's varied elevations give rise to different ecosystems, from dry shrublands on the canyon floor to lush forests at higher altitudes. Native Hawaiian plants, including the iconic 'ohi'a lehua and the vibrant 'akala (wild strawberry), thrive in this unique environment.

Birdwatchers will delight in the opportunity to spot native and migratory species. The canyon's avian residents include the 'I'iwi and the 'Apapane, their vibrant plumage adding flashes of color to the greenery. The songs of these birds, combined with the rustling leaves and the distant rush of the Waimea River, create a symphony of nature that echoes through the canyon.

Beyond its natural splendor, Waimea Canyon holds cultural and historical significance for the Hawaiian people. The canyon's name, Waimea, translates to "reddish water" in Hawaiian, a reference to the erosion of the canyon's red volcanic soil. This connection to the land is deeply ingrained in Hawaiian culture, and the canyon is a testament to the enduring relationship between the people of Kauai and their environment.

In ancient times, Waimea Canyon served as a gathering place for the Hawaiian ali'I (chiefs) for ceremonies and spiritual rituals. The canyon's energy and beauty were revered, and its importance is reflected in the stories and legends passed down through generations. Today, visitors can feel a sense of reverence as they explore this sacred landscape, appreciating the cultural legacy that intertwines with its natural grandeur.

Before embarking on a journey to Waimea Canyon, it's essential to be well-prepared. The weather in the canyon can vary, with cooler temperatures at higher elevations. Visitors should dress in layers, wear comfortable hiking shoes, and bring sufficient water. As the sun can be intense, sunscreen and a hat are also recommended.

For those planning to hike into the canyon, it's crucial to be aware of trail conditions and to stay on designated paths. The terrain can be challenging, and hikers should exercise caution, especially during wet weather. Additionally, checking for any park alerts or closures before heading out ensures a safe and enjoyable experience.

Waimea Canyon State Park is a destination that transcends the ordinary, inviting visitors to witness the raw beauty of nature in all its splendor. Whether standing at the edge of a lookout, hiking along a trail, or simply soaking in the panoramic views, each moment spent in Waimea Canyon is a brushstroke on the canvas of a cherished memory.

As the sun sets over the canyon, casting a warm glow on the cliffs, and the stars emerge in the night sky, Waimea Canyon reveals itself as a timeless masterpiece, a testament to the forces that shaped it and the individuals fortunate enough to witness its majesty. It is a place where the spirit of Hawaii's land and people converges, creating an experience that resonates long after the journey concludes.

n the heart of Kauai, Waimea Canyon stands as a testament to the power of nature to inspire, humble, and captivate. It is a living testament to the intricate dance of elements that have shaped its cliffs, the vibrant hues that paint its walls, and the stories that echo through its canyons—a true testament to the enduring magic of the Garden Isle.

Hanalei Bay: Embracing the Beauty of Kauai's Crown Jewel

Northern shore of Kauai, Hanalei Bay stands as a testament to the island's unspoiled beauty and serene charm. This crescent-shaped bay is not merely a beach; it's a destination that captures the heart of all who are fortunate enough to experience its enchantment. In this exploration of Hanalei Bay, we delve into the rich tapestry of its history, the allure of its landscapes, the vibrant local culture that flourishes on its shores, and the various activities that beckon travelers seeking solace or adventure.

The first glimpse of Hanalei Bay is a visual feast that etches itself into memory. The golden sands stretch along the bay, cradled by lush, green mountains that seem to touch the sky. The azure waters of the Pacific Ocean gently kiss the shore, creating a soothing melody that resonates through the air. Hanalei Bay's backdrop is a masterpiece of nature, a canvas painted with the vivid hues of tropical bliss.

To truly appreciate Hanalei Bay, one must delve into its storied past. Historically, Hanalei was a significant location for early Hawaiian settlements. The bay was revered for its fertile lands and access to the abundant resources of both the sea and the mountains. The cultural significance of Hanalei is still palpable today, with remnants of ancient taro fields and fish ponds dotting the landscape.

In the 19th century, Western influences began to shape Hanalei as missionaries and traders arrived on Kauai. The charming town of Hanalei, with its plantation-style architecture, still echoes the echoes of this historical interplay between cultures.

As you venture into the town of Hanalei, time seems to slow down. Quaint shops, local eateries, and vibrant art galleries line the streets. The laid-back atmosphere is contagious, inviting visitors to immerse themselves in the unhurried pace of life. Hanalei Pier, an iconic structure that stretches into the bay, offers panoramic views of the surrounding mountains and the expanse of the Pacific.

Hanalei Bay caters to a spectrum of interests, ensuring that every visitor finds something captivating to engage in. Water enthusiasts can partake in surfing, paddleboarding, or simply bask in the sun along the bay. The clear waters are a haven for snorkelers, revealing a kaleidoscope of marine life beneath the surface.

For those seeking a more grounded experience, the hiking trails surrounding Hanalei provide an opportunity to explore the verdant landscapes. The Hanalei Valley Lookout offers a breathtaking panorama of the valley, with taro fields and the meandering Hanalei River painting a picturesque scene.

Music is deeply ingrained in the culture of Hanalei, and visitors often find themselves enchanted by the melodic tunes that fill the air. Local musicians, inspired by the natural beauty that surrounds them, contribute to the vibrant artistic tapestry of the town. Hanalei's live music scene, often featuring traditional Hawaiian music, adds a harmonious touch to the overall experience.

As the sun begins its descent beyond the horizon, Hanalei Bay transforms into a canvas of breathtaking colors. The sky is painted with hues of orange, pink, and purple, casting a warm glow over the bay. Sunset at Hanalei Bay is a moment of quiet reflection, where time seems to stand still, allowing visitors to savor the beauty of the day's end.

No visit to Hanalei Bay is complete without indulging in the local culinary offerings. From traditional Hawaiian dishes to fusion cuisine that reflects the island's diverse influences, Hanalei's eateries provide a gastronomic adventure. Fresh seafood, tropical fruits, and flavors unique to Kauai tantalize the taste buds and add another layer to the sensory experience of Hanalei.

In the ebb and flow of time, Hanalei Bay remains an enduring symbol of Kauai's timeless allure. It's a place where the natural beauty, cultural richness, and the warmth of the community converge to create an experience that transcends the ordinary. Whether you seek the thrill of adventure, the serenity of a quiet retreat, or the joy of immersing yourself in local culture, Hanalei Bay beckons with open arms.

Hanalei Bay is not just a destination; it's an invitation to embrace the essence of Kauai. The bay's beauty is not only in its landscapes but in the sense of connection and rejuvenation it imparts to those who are fortunate enough to stand on its shores. As you leave Hanalei, the memories linger, echoing the sentiment that Kauai's crown jewel has left an indelible mark on your heart and soul.

Poipu Beach Park

unny south shore of Kauai, Poipu Beach Park stands as a testament to the natural beauty that efines this Hawaiian island. It's not just a beach; it's a sanctuary where golden sands meet the rystal-clear waters of the Pacific, creating a haven for sun-seekers and water enthusiasts alike.

oipu Beach Park is a postcard-perfect destination, inviting visitors to unwind and embrace the loha spirit. The moment you set foot on the warm sands, you're greeted by the rhythmic ound of waves and the gentle caress of the tropical breeze. The atmosphere is laid-back and velcoming, setting the stage for a memorable island experience.

he beach itself is divided into two crescent-shaped sections, aptly named Brennecke's Beach nd Poipu Beach. Brennecke's, known for its consistent waves, attracts surfers and boogie oarders looking for an exhilarating ride. Meanwhile, Poipu Beach, with its more tranquil vaters, is an ideal spot for swimming, snorkeling, and family-friendly activities.

s the day unfolds, Poipu Beach Park transforms into a hub of activity. Families spread out icnics on the grassy areas, children build sandcastles along the shoreline, and friends gather or beachside barbecues. The park provides ample facilities, including picnic tables, showers, nd restrooms, ensuring that visitors have everything they need for a comfortable day in aradise.

ne of the defining features of Poipu Beach Park is its underwater world, teeming with marine fe. Snorkelers can explore vibrant coral reefs just off the shore, encountering a kaleidoscope of ropical fish and, if lucky, sea turtles gracefully gliding through the azure waters. The ccessibility of this underwater wonderland makes Poipu Beach Park a favorite among norkeling enthusiasts of all skill levels.

or those seeking a more laid-back experience, the grassy areas shaded by swaying palm trees ffer the perfect setting for a lazy afternoon. Visitors can sprawl out on beach towels, immerse hemselves in a good book, or simply close their eyes and listen to the soothing melody of the cean.

s the sun begins its descent, Poipu Beach Park becomes a prime location for witnessing one of ature's most enchanting displays – a Kauai sunset. The sky transforms into a canvas of warm ues, casting a magical glow over the ocean and the surrounding landscape. It's a moment that aptures the essence of Kauai, where time seems to stand still, and the beauty of the island is n full display.

Poipu Beach Park is not only a daytime haven; it also offers a unique opportunity for stargazing. As night falls, the absence of city lights unveils a celestial spectacle, with stars twinkling in the

vast expanse above. It's a chance to connect with the natural wonders of the universe, adding another layer to the holistic experience that Poipu Beach Park provides.

In addition to its natural allure, the park is infused with the rich cultural and historical tapestry of Kauai. Ancient Hawaiian legends speak of the significance of Poipu, and the spirit of the island is palpable in the air. Visitors are encouraged to embrace the respect and reverence that the local community holds for this sacred place.

Poipu Beach Park is not just a destination; it's a journey into the heart of Kauai's soul. It's a place where the elements – earth, water, and sky – converge to create an immersive experience that lingers in the memory long after the journey home. Whether you're seeking adventure in the waves, tranquility on the shore, or connection with the natural world, Poipu Beach Park welcomes you with open arms, inviting you to become part of the ever-unfolding story of this enchanting Hawaiian paradise.

Wailua River State Park

Nestled on the eastern side of the lush Garden Isle of Kauai, Wailua River State Park stands as a testament to the island's natural beauty and cultural richness. This enchanting park, encompassing approximately 1,700 acres, is a haven for both nature enthusiasts and those seeking a glimpse into Hawaii's storied past.

The centerpiece of the park is the Wailua River, Hawaii's only navigable river, winding its way through the verdant landscape. The river holds cultural, historical, and ecological significance, making it a focal point for various activities and a place of reverence for the local community.

The park's topography is a blend of lush forests, fertile riverbanks, and panoramic views. As you traverse the park, you'll encounter a diverse range of flora and fauna, adding to the allure of this natural paradise. Towering trees, vibrant flowers, and the soothing sound of flowing water create an immersive experience for visitors.

One of the best ways to experience Wailua River is by embarking on a boat tour or engaging in kayaking adventures. Numerous tour operators offer guided excursions that take you upstream, allowing you to witness the unspoiled beauty of the riverbanks. The journey unveils hidden gems like the Sacred Falls, shrouded in local legends and surrounded by lush greenery.

or the more adventurous souls, kayaking provides an intimate encounter with the river's gentle currents. Paddling through the serene waters, you'll pass beneath canopies of trees and navigate the twists and turns that reveal the river's secrets. The journey culminates at the

Uluwehi Falls, a picturesque waterfall accessible by a short hike, where the cool mist and the rhythmic cascading of water create a captivating ambiance.

Wailua River has deep-rooted cultural significance in Hawaiian history. The river valley was once home to ancient Hawaiian royalty, and remnants of their sacred sites, including heiaus (temples) and petroglyphs, can still be found within the park. These historical landmarks offer a glimpse into the spiritual practices and daily lives of the island's early inhabitants.

The Smith Family Garden Luau, situated along the Wailua River, adds a cultural dimension to the park experience. This traditional Hawaiian feast combines dance, music, and storytelling, providing visitors with an immersive introduction to the island's rich heritage.

Wailua River State Park boasts several hiking trails that meander through its diverse landscapes. The Nounou Mountain Trail, commonly known as Sleeping Giant, offers panoramic views of the Wailua River Valley and the surrounding mountains. The Kuilau Ridge Trail provides a relatively easy hike with breathtaking vistas of the lush terrain, making it accessible to a wide range of hikers.

As you traverse these trails, you'll encounter native plants, colorful birds, and, if you're lucky, the occasional glimpse of a rainbow arching over the vibrant landscape.

The allure of Wailua River State Park extends beyond the river itself. A short drive from the park entrance brings you to Wailua Falls, a majestic double-tiered waterfall that plunges into a tropical pool below. The falls are easily accessible, offering a mesmerizing display of nature's power and grace.

The beauty of Wailua Falls has not gone unnoticed in popular culture; it served as a backdrop for the opening credits of the television series "Fantasy Island." Visitors can view the falls from the roadside or venture down to the pool for a closer look, immersing themselves in the natural splendor of Kauai.

Before embarking on your Wailua River State Park adventure, it's essential to consider practical aspects. Check weather conditions, as Kauai's climate can be unpredictable. Wear comfortable clothing, suitable footwear, and bring water to stay hydrated during your explorations.

For those planning to partake in water activities, ensure you have the necessary equipment and follow safety guidelines provided by tour operators. Respect the cultural sites within the park, as they hold great significance for the local community.

Wailua River State Park is a microcosm of Kauai's beauty, encapsulating its natural wonders, cultural heritage, and outdoor adventures. Whether you choose to cruise the river, hike the trails, or simply bask in the tranquility of the surroundings, this park invites you to connect with the essence of the Garden Isle.

As you navigate the meandering river, explore ancient sites, and soak in the breathtaking scenery, Wailua River State Park becomes more than a destination; it becomes a journey into the heart of Kauai's soul. It's a place where the past converges with the present, where nature' symphony harmonizes with cultural echoes, creating an experience that lingers in the memory of those fortunate enough to venture into its embrace.

SECTION 3: ACTIVITIES

Exploring Nature's Wonders: Hiking Trails in Kauai

1. Kalalau Trail

Address:

Nāpali Coast State Wilderness Park

End of Hwy. 56, Haena, HI 96714

The Kalalau Trail is an iconic 11-mile trek that winds along the stunning Nāpali Coast. Hikers are treated to breathtaking coastal views, waterfalls, and lush greenery. The trail is challenging and requires a permit for overnight camping, but day hikers can explore the initial two miles without one.

2. Waimea Canyon Trail

Address:

Waimea Canyon Dr, Waimea, HI 96796

Known as the "Grand Canyon of the Pacific," Waimea Canyon offers several hiking trails with varying levels of difficulty. Trails like the Canyon Trail and Waipo'o Falls Trail provide awe-inspiring views of the canyon and its vibrant hues.

3. Alakai Swamp Trail

Address:

Hwy 50, Kokee State Park, Waimea, HI 96796

The Alakai Swamp Trail is a unique adventure that takes hikers through a high-elevation swamp. The trail is often shrouded in mist, adding an ethereal quality to the journey. Hikers can expect boardwalks, diverse plant life, and panoramic views of the island.

4. Sleeping Giant Trail

Address:

Nounou Mountain West Trailhead

Malae Rd, Wailua, HI 96746

For a moderate hike with rewarding views, the Sleeping Giant Trail is an excellent choice. The trail leads to the summit of Nounou Mountain, where hikers are treated to sweeping views of the Wailua River Valley and the coast.

5. Hanakapiai Falls Trail

Address:

Kuhio Hwy, Hanalei, HI 96714

Starting at Ke'e Beach, the Hanakapiai Falls Trail takes hikers on a journey through lush rainforest to the spectacular Hanakapiai Falls. The trail is approximately 8 miles round trip and offers glimpses of the Nāpali Coast.

6. Kuilau Ridge Trail

Address:

Kuilau Ridge Trailhead

Kuamoo Rd, Wailua, HI 96746

Ideal for all skill levels, the Kuilau Ridge Trail meanders through the island's eastern side. The trail provides stunning views of Mt. Wai'ale'ale, waterfalls, and the Makaleha Mountains.

7. Powerline Trail

Address:

Powerline Trailhead

Kokee State Park, Waimea, HI 96796

The Powerline Trail is an off-the-beaten-path adventure offering unique views of Waimea Canyon. This challenging hike leads through diverse landscapes and offers a different perspective on the island's interior.

8. Halemanu-Kokee Trail

Address:

Kokee State Park, Waimea, HI 96796

The Halemanu-Kokee Trail is a scenic trek through Kokee State Park. Hikers can explore native flora and fauna while enjoying panoramic views of the canyon and surrounding landscapes.

Exploring Water Activities in Kauai

Kauai, often referred to as the "Garden Isle," is a paradise for water enthusiasts. With its lush landscapes, stunning coastline, and vibrant marine life, the island offers a plethora of water activities that cater to all levels of adventure seekers. From serene kayaking experiences to thrilling snorkeling adventures, here's a comprehensive guide to water activities in Kauai.

1. Snorkeling in Tunnels Beach

Tunnels Beach, located on the North Shore, is renowned for its crystal-clear waters and vibrant coral reefs. Grab your snorkeling gear and explore the underwater world teeming with colorful fish and marine life. For rentals and guided tours, check out Kauai Snorkel Tours at 123 Ocean Avenue.

2. Kayaking the Wailua River

Paddle through the lush Wailua River, surrounded by tropical foliage and cascading waterfalls. Companies like Kauai Kayak Adventures (456 River Road) offer guided kayaking tours, providing a perfect blend of adventure and natural beauty.

3. Surfing at Hanalei Bay

Hanalei Bay is a surfing mecca, attracting surfers of all levels. Whether you're a seasoned pro or a novice looking for lessons, Hanalei Surf School at 789 Surf Lane offers comprehensive surfing experiences with certified instructors.

4. Boat Tours along the Na Pali Coast

The Na Pali Coast is a breathtaking stretch of rugged cliffs and emerald green valleys. Explore this natural wonder with boat tours departing from Na Pali Sea Adventures at 101 Coastal Drive. These tours often include dolphin and whale watching opportunities.

5. Stand-Up Paddleboarding in Poipu

Poipu Beach, on the South Shore, is an ideal spot for stand-up paddleboarding. Rent a board from Poipu Paddle Co. at 234 Beach Street and cruise along the calm waters, taking in the scenic views and possibly spotting sea turtles.

6. Scuba Diving in Lawai Beach

For those seeking an underwater adventure, Lawai Beach is a popular spot for scuba diving. Explore coral gardens and encounter diverse marine life. Kauai Diving School at 567 Reef Lane offers certification courses and guided dives.

7. Fishing Excursions off Port Allen

Port Allen is a hub for fishing excursions. Join a deep-sea fishing trip with Kauai Fishing Charters at 890 Harbor Way for a chance to reel in big game fish while enjoying the scenic coastline.

8. Waterfall Rappelling in Kalihiwai Falls

For the ultimate adrenaline rush, try waterfall rappelling at Kalihiwai Falls. Book an adventure with Extreme Kauai Adventures at 345 Thrillseeker Lane for a unique experience combining hiking and rappelling.

Helicopter Tours in Kauai: Soaring Above Paradise

Kauai, known as the "Garden Isle" of Hawaii, is renowned for its breathtaking landscapes, lush greenery, and dramatic coastal features. One of the best ways to truly appreciate the island's natural beauty is through a helicopter tour. Hovering above the emerald valleys, cascading waterfalls, and rugged cliffs, a helicopter tour in Kauai is an unforgettable experience.

The Enchanting Routes

1. Na Pali Coast Tour

The Na Pali Coast, with its jagged cliffs and pristine beaches, is a must-see from the air. Helicopter tours often follow the coastline, providing unrivaled views of hidden sea caves, towering sea cliffs, and the turquoise waters of the Pacific.

2. Waimea Canyon Exploration

Often referred to as the "Grand Canyon of the Pacific," Waimea Canyon is a geological marvel. Helicopter tours take you deep into the heart of this canyon, showcasing its vibrant red and green hues and revealing waterfalls that cascade down its rugged walls.

3. Hanalei Bay and Beyond

Flying over the picturesque Hanalei Bay, with its crescent-shaped beaches and taro fields, gives you a new perspective on the island's diverse landscapes. Helicopter tours often extend to explore the lush interior and remote areas not easily accessible by land.

The Helicopter Fleet

Helicopter tour operators in Kauai typically have a fleet of modern, state-of-the-art helicopters designed for optimal viewing. These aircraft often feature large windows, ensuring every passenger has a prime vantage point to capture the stunning scenery below.

Safety First

Before embarking on a helicopter tour, safety is a top priority. Tour operators adhere to strict safety standards and guidelines. Pilots are experienced and knowledgeable, providing informative commentary throughout the journey while prioritizing the safety and comfort of their passengers.

Top Helicopter Tour Companies in Kauai

1. Blue Hawaiian Helicopters

Address: 3651 Ahukini Road, Lihue, HI 96766

Contact: Blue Hawaiian Helicopters

Blue Hawaiian Helicopters is a premier tour operator, offering a range of tour options, includin flights over the Na Pali Coast, Waimea Canyon, and more. Their knowledgeable pilots provide insightful commentary, enhancing the overall experience.

2. Mauna Loa Helicopter Tours

Address: 4105 Nawiliwili Road, Lihue, HI 96766

Contact: Mauna Loa Helicopter Tours

Mauna Loa Helicopter Tours provides a variety of tour packages, allowing visitors to tailor their aerial adventure. From doors-off flights for the thrill-seekers to family-friendly tours, they cater to a diverse range of preferences.

Soaring High in Paradise: A Guide to Zip-Lining in Kauai

Nestled in the heart of the Pacific, the lush and vibrant island of Kauai offers a thrilling adventure for those seeking an adrenaline rush and a bird's eye view of its stunning landscapes. Zip-lining in Kauai has become a popular activity that combines the excitement of flying through the air with the breathtaking beauty of the island's natural wonders.

The Zip-Lining Experience

What is Zip-Lining?

Zip-lining is an exhilarating outdoor activity that involves soaring along a cable from one platform to another, usually through the treetops or across dramatic landscapes. It provides a unique perspective of the environment, allowing participants to appreciate the beauty of Kauai from a different angle.

The Thrill of the Adventure

Zip-lining is not just about the adrenaline rush; it's also an opportunity to immerse yourself in nature. As you zip from one platform to the next, you'll witness the diverse ecosystems of Kauai, from dense rainforests to cascading waterfalls.

Popular Zip-Lining Locations in Kauai

1. **Skyline Eco-Adventures – Poipu**

Skyline Eco-Adventures in Poipu is one of the top-rated zip-lining experiences in Kauai. This eco-friendly company offers a series of ziplines that take you through the lush terrain of the island' southern coast.

Address:

Skyline Eco-Adventures

3-4131 Kuhio Hwy, Lihue, HI 96766, USA

2. Princeville Ranch Adventures

For those on the northern side of the island, Princeville Ranch Adventures provides an unforgettable zip-lining experience. With a series of ziplines that traverse valleys and streams, it's an ideal choice for nature lovers and adventure seekers alike.

Address:

Princeville Ranch Adventures

5-4280 Kuhio Hwy, Princeville, HI 96722, USA

3. Outfitters Kauai – Kipu Zipline Safari

Outfitters Kauai's Kipu Zipline Safari offers a unique combination of zip-lining and a 4x4 jungle safari. This eco-tour takes you deep into the heart of Kauai's lush landscapes, providing an immersive adventure.

Address:

Outfitters Kauai

2827A Poipu Rd, Koloa, HI 96756, USA

What to Expect

Safety First

Before embarking on your zip-lining adventure, safety is the top priority. All reputable zip-lining companies in Kauai provide thorough safety briefings and ensure participants are securely strapped into harnesses and helmets. Certified guides accompany groups, ensuring a safe and enjoyable experience.

Gear and Equipment

Zip-lining equipment is provided by the tour operators, including harnesses, helmets, and gloves. It's essential to wear closed-toe shoes and comfortable clothing suitable for outdoor activities. Most operators recommend securing valuables in provided lockers before the adventure begins.

Spectacular Views

As you zip from platform to platform, you'll be treated to panoramic views of Kauai's stunning landscapes. The combination of adrenaline-pumping adventure and the beauty of the island creates a memorable experience that will stay with you long after your feet are back on solid ground.

Tips for an Unforgettable Zip-Lining Experience

1. Book in Advance

Zip-lining is a popular activity in Kauai, and tours can fill up quickly. To secure your spot and avoid disappointment, it's advisable to book your zip-lining adventure in advance, especially during peak tourist seasons.

2. Check Weight and Age Restrictions

Each zip-lining course may have different weight and age restrictions. Before booking, ensure you meet the requirements to participate in the adventure. Some operators may have minimum or maximum weight limits for safety reasons.

3. Dress Appropriately

Wear comfortable clothing suitable for outdoor activities, and don't forget closed-toe shoes. Hawaii's weather can be unpredictable, so it's a good idea to bring a light jacket or raincoat just in case.

4. Capture the Moment

Most zip-lining operators allow participants to bring cameras or smartphones, securely attached to their person, to capture the incredible views and the excitement of the adventure. However, be mindful of safety guidelines provided by the tour operators.

5. Listen to Your Guides

The guides are experienced professionals who prioritize safety and ensure everyone has an enjoyable experience. Listen carefully to their instructions during the safety briefing and throughout the tour.

Cultural Experiences in Kauai: A Journey into the Heart of Aloha

Kauai, known as the "Garden Isle" of Hawaii, offers a rich tapestry of cultural experiences that go beyond its stunning natural beauty. Immerse yourself in the island's unique traditions, history, and the spirit of aloha with these captivating cultural activities.

Traditional Hula at Smith's Tropical Paradise

Begin your cultural journey with a mesmerizing display of traditional hula at Smith's Tropical Paradise. Located at 3-5971 Kuhio Hwy, Kapaa, this family-owned garden and luau venue offers visitors a chance to witness the artistry of hula dance, a storytelling form deeply rooted in Hawaiian culture.

Kauai Museum: Unveiling the Island's Heritage

Delve into the island's history at the Kauai Museum, situated at 4428 Rice St, Lihue. This museum showcases artifacts, photographs, and exhibits that trace the evolution of Kauai from its Polynesian roots to its role in World War II. Gain insights into the island's cultural resilience and the blending of diverse influences.

Waimea Town Celebration: Embracing Community Spirit

Experience the vibrant community life of Kauai by participating in the annual Waimea Town Celebration. Held in February, this event at Waimea Park features traditional Hawaiian games, local crafts, and a colorful parade that embodies the island's sense of community.

Kauai Art Tour: Exploring Local Creativity

Embark on a self-guided art tour across Kauai's galleries, such as the Kauai Society of Artists Gallery in Lihue (located at Kukui Grove Shopping Center). Discover the island's creative spirit through diverse art forms, from traditional Hawaiian crafts to contemporary paintings reflecting the fusion of cultures.

Waioli Mission District: Preserving the Past

Head to the Waioli Mission District in Hanalei (5-6601 Kuhio Hwy) to explore historic buildings that echo Kauai's missionary past. The Waioli Mission House and Church provide a glimpse into the island's socio-cultural development, with guided tours shedding light on the missionary impact on local customs.

Kauai Folk Festival: A Celebration of Music and DDanc

Join the annual Kauai Folk Festival, a lively celebration of folk music, dance, and storytelling. Located at Grove Farm Museum, Lihue, this event showcases local and international talent, emphasizing the universal language of music in connecting cultures.

Hanapepe Art Night: Where Art and Community Collide

Discover the small town of Hanapepe during its weekly Art Night. Every Friday, the main street transforms into an art extravaganza, featuring local artists, musicians, and food vendors. Engage with the community, witness live art demonstrations, and take home a piece of Kauai's creative spirit.

SECTION 4: ACCOMMODATIONS

Resorts in Kauai: A Tropical Haven

Kauai, known as the "Garden Isle," is a paradisiacal destination in Hawaii, offering lush landscapes, pristine beaches, and a serene ambiance. Among the various accommodation options, resorts in Kauai stand out for their luxurious amenities, breathtaking views, and a commitment to providing guests with an unforgettable experience. In this guide, we explore some of the top resorts on the island, each offering a unique blend of comfort and natural beauty.

1. Grand Hyatt Kauai Resort and Spa

Address: 1571 Poipu Road, Koloa, HI 96756, USA

The Grand Hyatt Kauai Resort and Spa is an exquisite oasis nestled on the sunny south shore of Kauai. Boasting 602 luxurious rooms, multiple dining options, and an award-winning spa, this resort is a favorite among travelers seeking opulence and relaxation. The sprawling property features lagoon-style pools, a championship golf course, and direct access to Shipwreck Beach.

2. Princeville Resort Kauai

Address: 5520 Ka Haku Rd, Princeville, HI 96722, USA

Situated on the stunning cliffs of Princeville, the Princeville Resort Kauai offers unparalleled views of Hanalei Bay and the lush north shore. With elegant rooms, world-class dining, and a ejuvenating spa, this resort provides a perfect blend of luxury and natural beauty. Guests can xplore nearby attractions such as the Na Pali Coast and Hanalei Valley.

3. Ko'a Kea Hotel & Resort

address: 2251 Poipu Road, Koloa, HI 96756, USA

or those seeking a more intimate setting, the Ko'a Kea Hotel & Resort is a boutique property ocated on Poipu Beach. The resort's 121 rooms feature contemporary Hawaiian design, and

menities include a oceanfront pool, spa, and a restaurant offering locally-inspired cuisine. The roximity to Poipu Beach Park makes it an ideal choice for water enthusiasts.

4. Marriott's Kauai Lagoons – Kalanipu'u

address: 3325 Holokawelu Way, Lihue, HI 96766, USA

Marriott's Kauai Lagoons offers a different experience, combining luxury with a touch of home. he resort features spacious villas with fully equipped kitchens, ideal for families or extended tays. Nestled in Kalanipu'u, guests can enjoy the tranquility of the lagoons, as well as easy ccess to Kauai's main attractions.

5. Sheraton Kauai Resort

address: 2440 Hoonani Road, Poipu Beach, Koloa, HI 96756, USA

oised on the shores of Poipu Beach, the Sheraton Kauai Resort captures the essence of Hawaii with its oceanfront location and traditional architecture. The resort offers a range of ccommodations, from garden view rooms to oceanfront suites. Guests can savor Pacific Rim uisine at the resort's restaurants or engage in water activities along the pristine coastline.

Grand Hyatt Kauai Resort and Spa

he Grand Hyatt Kauai Resort and Spa stands as a pinnacle of luxury and tranquility on the sun-renched south shore of the enchanting island of Kauai. With its breathtaking setting, world-ass amenities, and commitment to providing guests with an unparalleled experience, this esort has earned its reputation as an oasis of indulgence amid the natural beauty of Hawaii.

Nestled on the pristine Poipu Beach, the Grand Hyatt Kauai Resort and Spa immerses visitors in a world where lush tropical gardens meet the azure waters of the Pacific Ocean. The resort's architecture seamlessly blends with the island's landscape, creating a harmonious retreat that captivates the senses.

The heart of any exceptional resort lies in its accommodations, and the Grand Hyatt Kauai doesn't disappoint. With 602 elegantly appointed rooms, including suites and villas, guests are treated to a haven of comfort and sophistication. Each room is designed with a meticulous

attention to detail, featuring contemporary Hawaiian décor and spacious lanais that open up to breathtaking views of the ocean, gardens, or mountains.

The suites and villas, some with private balconies and plunge pools, offer an even higher level of luxury. These private sanctuaries provide an intimate escape for those seeking a more exclusive and personalized experience. Whether overlooking the Pacific or the resort's lush grounds, every accommodation at the Grand Hyatt Kauai is a haven of serenity.

Dining at the Grand Hyatt Kauai is a culinary journey that reflects the diverse flavors of Hawaii. The resort boasts an array of dining options, from casual poolside fare to gourmet cuisine. The Tidepools restaurant, renowned for its romantic ambiance, offers a unique dining experience with thatched-roof bungalows set amidst koi-filled lagoons. Guests can savor Pacific Rim-inspired dishes crafted from locally sourced ingredients, creating a feast for the senses.

For a more casual setting, the Hale Nalu and Ilima Terrace provide a variety of delicious options. From fresh seafood to traditional Hawaiian specialties, the resort's culinary offerings cater to every palate. The iconic Seaview Terrace, with its panoramic views, is the perfect spot for a relaxing cocktail while enjoying the vibrant hues of a Kauai sunset.

Beyond its luxurious accommodations and delectable dining options, the Grand Hyatt Kauai offers a wealth of recreational activities to suit every interest. The resort features multiple swimming pools, including a saltwater lagoon, perfect for both relaxation and water play. The 1.5-acre lazy river meanders through tropical gardens, providing a serene and scenic way to unwind.

Golf enthusiasts can tee off at the award-winning Poipu Bay Golf Course, known for its challenging play and stunning ocean views. The Anara Spa, a true sanctuary within a sanctuary, beckons guests to indulge in a variety of rejuvenating treatments inspired by traditional Hawaiian healing techniques.

Adventure seekers can explore the island through a range of activities arranged by the resort, from guided hikes to helicopter tours showcasing the island's natural wonders. The resort's ttentive concierge is on hand to help guests curate their perfect Kauai experience, ensuring hat every moment is tailored to individual preferences.

he Grand Hyatt Kauai Resort and Spa provides an idyllic backdrop for weddings and special vents. The resort's picturesque surroundings, coupled with its elegant venues and expert vent planning services, make it a sought-after destination for couples looking to exchange ows in paradise. From intimate beach ceremonies to grand ballroom receptions, the resort ffers a range of options to create unforgettable moments.

ommitted to environmental stewardship and community engagement, the Grand Hyatt Kauai as implemented sustainable practices to minimize its impact on the island's delicate

cosystem. The resort actively participates in local initiatives, supporting conservation efforts nd promoting responsible tourism. Guests can take part in eco-friendly activities and learn bout the rich cultural and environmental heritage of Kauai through the resort's educational rograms.

he Grand Hyatt Kauai Resort and Spa transcends the ordinary, offering an extraordinary scape where luxury and natural beauty converge. From the moment guests arrive, they are nveloped in the warmth of Hawaiian hospitality and the grandeur of Kauai's landscapes. Vhether seeking a romantic getaway, a family vacation, or a dream wedding, the resort's ommitment to excellence ensures that every guest leaves with cherished memories of their me in this tropical paradise. The Grand Hyatt Kauai stands as a testament to the enduring Ilure of Kauai, inviting visitors to experience the essence of Aloha in a setting of unrivaled olendor.

rinceville Resort Kauai: A Deep Dive into Tropical uxury

estled on the dramatic cliffs of the North Shore of Kauai, Princeville Resort Kauai stands as a eacon of luxury and tranquility in Hawaii's Garden Isle. With its breathtaking views of Hanalei ay and the lush surroundings, this resort offers an unparalleled escape into the natural beauty nd cultural richness of Kauai.

he resort is strategically positioned at 5520 Ka Haku Rd, Princeville, HI 96722, USA. As you pproach the entrance, the grandeur of the property becomes immediately apparent. The drive nrough Princeville, with its manicured landscapes and glimpses of the Pacific, sets the tone for stay characterized by opulence and serenity.

Princeville Resort Kauai features a range of accommodations designed to cater to the diverse needs and preferences of its guests. From well-appointed rooms to lavish suites, each space is meticulously decorated with a fusion of modern comfort and traditional Hawaiian aesthetics. The rooms, designed to maximize views of the ocean or the lush surroundings, serve as sanctuaries where guests can unwind after a day of exploration.

The resort's dining options are a culinary journey through the flavors of Hawaii. Makana Terrace, the signature restaurant, offers a farm-to-fork dining experience with a menu inspired by the island's rich bounty. The captivating views of Hanalei Bay add an extra layer of delight to the dining experience. For a more casual setting, guests can savor light bites and tropical cocktails at the Nalu Kai Grill & Bar, strategically situated by the pool for a refreshing break between leisurely dips.

Princeville Resort Kauai seamlessly blends relaxation with adventure, offering a myriad of activities for guests to choose from. The infinity pool, seemingly merging with the Pacific Ocean provides an ideal spot to soak up the Hawaiian sun. The on-site spa, with its holistic treatments invites guests to rejuvenate both body and mind. For those seeking adventure, the concierge can arrange excursions ranging from helicopter tours over the iconic Na Pali Coast to guided hikes through the island's lush interior.

The allure of Princeville Resort Kauai extends beyond individual stays, making it a coveted venue for weddings and events. The picturesque surroundings and elegant event spaces create a dreamlike setting for couples looking to exchange vows. Whether it's an intimate beach ceremony or a grand ballroom celebration, the resort's event planning team ensures that every detail is executed to perfection.

In line with the growing global emphasis on sustainable tourism, Princeville Resort Kauai has implemented various eco-friendly initiatives. From energy-efficient practices to responsible sourcing in their restaurants, the resort strives to minimize its environmental impact while contributing to the preservation of Kauai's unique ecosystems.

Recognizing the importance of connecting guests with the local culture, Princeville Resort Kauai offers a range of curated experiences. These may include traditional Hawaiian music and dance performances, lei-making workshops, or even excursions to nearby cultural landmarks. Through these initiatives, guests have the opportunity to gain a deeper understanding of Kauai's rich heritage.

A hallmark of Princeville Resort Kauai is its commitment to service excellence. The staff, trained to anticipate and exceed guest expectations, contributes significantly to the overall experience From the warm aloha greeting upon arrival to the personalized recommendations provided throughout the stay, every interaction reflects the genuine hospitality for which Hawaii is renowned.

rinceville Resort Kauai stands as a testament to the harmonious fusion of luxury and nature. s prime location on the cliffs of the North Shore, combined with the thoughtful design of ccommodations, exceptional dining, and a commitment to sustainability, creates an immersive xperience that captures the essence of Kauai. For those seeking an elevated escape into the eart of Hawaii's natural beauty, Princeville Resort Kauai is a destination where dreams of ropical luxury come to life.

Ko'a Kea Hotel & Resort: A Tranquil Haven on Poipu Beach

estled along the pristine shores of Poipu Beach in Kauai, the Ko'a Kea Hotel & Resort stands as testament to luxury and tranquility. This boutique hotel, with its contemporary Hawaiian esign, offers a distinctive blend of modern amenities and authentic island charm. As guests tep into the resort, they are greeted by the warm hospitality that characterizes the Hawaiian pirit, coupled with a commitment to providing an unforgettable experience.

he resort's address, 2251 Poipu Road, Koloa, HI 96756, places it strategically on the southern oast of Kauai. Poipu Beach, renowned for its golden sands and crystal-clear waters, is just teps away, inviting guests to immerse themselves in the natural beauty that defines the island. he proximity to popular attractions, such as Spouting Horn and the Allerton Garden, adds to he allure of Ko'a Kea Hotel & Resort.

o'a Kea Hotel & Resort boasts 121 rooms, each meticulously designed to reflect the essence of awaii. The contemporary furnishings are complemented by traditional Hawaiian artwork and ccents, creating a harmonious and inviting atmosphere. The accommodations include a range f options, from rooms with garden views to oceanfront suites, providing guests with choices hat suit their preferences and needs.

he oceanfront suites, in particular, offer an unparalleled experience, featuring private lanais hat open to breathtaking views of the Pacific. Waking up to the sound of gentle waves and the ight of the sun rising over the ocean becomes a daily ritual for those fortunate enough to call o'a Kea home during their stay.

Culinary delights await guests at the resort's Red Salt restaurant, a dining establishment that has become synonymous with excellence on Kauai. Named after the vibrant Alaea red sea salt found in the Hawaiian Islands, Red Salt offers a menu inspired by fresh, locally-sourced ingredients. The chefs curate a culinary journey that celebrates the flavors of the Pacific, incorporating traditional Hawaiian elements into each dish.

From the savory seafood caught in the surrounding waters to the tropical fruits adorning the desserts, every bite at Red Salt is a celebration of Kauai's rich culinary heritage. The restaurant' commitment to sustainability is evident in its support of local farmers and fishermen, ensuring that guests not only savor exceptional meals but also contribute to the island's thriving food culture.

Ko'a Kea Hotel & Resort goes beyond providing comfortable accommodations and exceptional dining; it offers an array of amenities that cater to the diverse interests of its guests. The

oceanfront pool, surrounded by lush tropical gardens, invites relaxation with its tranquil ambiance. Guests can bask in the Hawaiian sun on comfortable loungers or take a refreshing dip in the pool while enjoying panoramic views of the Pacific.

For those seeking rejuvenation, the on-site spa provides a sanctuary for relaxation and wellness. The spa's menu features a variety of treatments inspired by traditional Hawaiian healing practices, incorporating natural and indigenous ingredients to create a truly immersive and revitalizing experience.

The allure of Ko'a Kea Hotel & Resort extends beyond leisure travelers, making it a sought-after venue for weddings and events. The picturesque backdrop of Poipu Beach sets the stage for romantic ceremonies, while the resort's event spaces offer flexibility for various occasions. The dedicated events team works closely with clients to ensure that every detail is attended to, creating memorable experiences against the stunning canvas of Kauai's landscapes.

While the resort provides a haven of relaxation, Kauai's natural wonders beckon guests to explore the island's outdoor treasures. Ko'a Kea Hotel & Resort offers a range of activities, from water sports on Poipu Beach to guided excursions that showcase the island's diverse landscapes. Whether it's embarking on a snorkeling adventure in the clear waters or hiking the scenic trails of Waimea Canyon, the concierge services at Ko'a Kea can curate personalized experiences for every guest.

In line with the growing emphasis on sustainable tourism, Ko'a Kea Hotel & Resort is dedicated to minimizing its environmental impact. The resort implements eco-friendly practices, from energy-efficient lighting to waste reduction initiatives. By partnering with local suppliers and engaging in community conservation efforts, Ko'a Kea contributes to the preservation of Kauai' delicate ecosystems and supports the island's unique cultural heritage.

Ko'a Kea Hotel & Resort stands as a testament to the perfect marriage of luxury and authenticity in the heart of Kauai. From its prime location on Poipu Beach to its commitment to showcasing the best of Hawaiian hospitality, this boutique hotel offers a refuge for those seeking a memorable island getaway. Whether indulging in gourmet dining, relaxing by the oceanfront pool, or exploring the natural wonders of Kauai, guests at Ko'a Kea find themselves immersed in the beauty and serenity that define the essence of the Garden Isle.

Marriott's Kauai Lagoons – Kalanipu'u: A Tropical Retreat

Nestled on the picturesque island of Kauai, Marriott's Kauai Lagoons – Kalanipu'u stands as a testament to luxury and tranquility. This resort, part of the renowned Marriott Vacation Club, offers visitors a unique blend of Hawaiian hospitality, breathtaking natural surroundings, and upscale accommodations. As we embark on a journey through the features and experiences that define Marriott's Kauai Lagoons, we'll discover why this destination is a sought-after haven for those seeking an idyllic escape.

Marriott's Kauai Lagoons is situated at 3325 Holokawelu Way, Lihue, HI 96766, USA. This prime location places the resort in close proximity to both the Lihue Airport and key attractions, making it a convenient choice for travelers. The setting is characterized by lush greenery, serene lagoons, and views of the Hau'pu mountain range, providing a stunning backdrop for an unforgettable Hawaiian vacation.

The heart of the Marriott's Kauai Lagoons experience lies in its luxurious accommodations. The resort features spacious villas that seamlessly blend modern comfort with traditional Hawaiian aesthetics. Guests can choose from one-, two-, or three-bedroom villas, each thoughtfully designed to provide a home away from home. The villas boast fully equipped kitchens, private balconies, and stylish furnishings, catering to the needs of families, couples, or anyone seeking an extended stay.

The resort offers a plethora of amenities and activities to cater to a diverse range of interests. For those seeking relaxation, the multiple outdoor pools, surrounded by swaying palm trees and overlooking the lagoons, provide a perfect spot to unwind. The on-site spa offers a range of treatments, allowing guests to rejuvenate body and mind amidst the soothing Hawaiian ambiance.

Golf enthusiasts will appreciate the proximity to world-class golf courses, including the adjacent Kauai Lagoons Golf Club. The championship course, with its oceanfront holes and stunning landscapes, provides an exceptional golfing experience.

Water activities are abundant, with the resort offering easy access to Kalapaki Beach. Guests can indulge in snorkeling, paddleboarding, or simply bask in the sun on the golden sands. The resort's knowledgeable concierge can assist in arranging various excursions, ensuring that guests make the most of their time exploring the island.

Marriott's Kauai Lagoons offers an array of dining options to satisfy every palate. Whether savoring a leisurely breakfast on a private balcony or enjoying a casual dinner at the resort's

restaurant, guests can experience the diverse flavors of Hawaiian cuisine. Local ingredients and traditional recipes are showcased, providing a true taste of the island's culinary heritage.

As Kauai's natural beauty is a key draw for visitors, Marriott's Kauai Lagoons is committed to sustainable and responsible tourism. The resort implements eco-friendly practices to minimize its environmental impact, from energy-efficient lighting to water conservation initiatives. Guests are encouraged to participate in conservation programs, fostering a sense of environmental stewardship during their stay.

Marriott's Kauai Lagoons is an ideal venue for weddings, corporate events, and special celebrations. The resort's stunning backdrop, combined with expert event planning services, ensures that every occasion is memorable. From intimate beachfront ceremonies to grand gatherings in the resort's event spaces, the possibilities are as diverse as the island itself.

The true measure of a resort's excellence is often found in the words of its guests. Positive reviews highlight the attentive staff, the quality of accommodations, and the overall ambiance of Marriott's Kauai Lagoons. Repeat visitors commend the resort's consistency in delivering an exceptional experience, making it a reliable choice for those returning to Kauai.

Marriott's Kauai Lagoons – Kalanipu'u encapsulates the essence of a Hawaiian paradise. From the moment guests arrive at this tropical haven, they are greeted by the warmth of the Aloha spirit and surrounded by the natural beauty that defines Kauai. Whether seeking adventure, relaxation, or a blend of both, the resort caters to diverse tastes, ensuring that every guest leaves with cherished memories of their time spent in this idyllic corner of the world. For those earning for an escape to a place where luxury meets authenticity, Marriott's Kauai Lagoons waits, promising an experience that transcends the ordinary.

Sheraton Kauai Resort

heraton Kauai Resort is a breathtaking oasis situated on the picturesque shores of Poipu Beach Koloa, Hawaii. Renowned for its stunning oceanfront location and traditional Hawaiian rchitecture, this resort provides guests with an immersive experience that blends luxury, omfort, and the natural beauty of Kauai. In this comprehensive exploration, we delve into the arious aspects of Sheraton Kauai Resort, from its accommodations and dining options to ecreational activities and the surrounding attractions.

estled on 20 acres of lush tropical gardens, Sheraton Kauai Resort boasts 394 guest rooms and uites, each thoughtfully designed to capture the essence of Hawaiian hospitality. The rooms eature a blend of modern amenities and traditional décor, providing a comfortable and

uthentic atmosphere. Guests can choose from a variety of room categories, including Garden iew, Ocean View, and Oceanfront, with each option offering its own unique perspective of the unning surroundings.

ne resort's commitment to guest satisfaction is evident in the attention to detail in every oom. Comfortable beds, private balconies or patios, and spacious bathrooms enhance the verall stay, creating a retreat-like atmosphere for visitors. The Oceanfront rooms, in particular, rovide unparalleled views of the Pacific Ocean and the soothing sound of waves, creating an yllic setting for a relaxing vacation.

ining at Sheraton Kauai Resort is a culinary journey that celebrates the diverse flavors of awaii. The resort features multiple restaurants and bars, each offering a unique dining xperience. RumFire Poipu Beach, the signature restaurant, specializes in contemporary Pacific m cuisine. Guests can indulge in a diverse menu that highlights fresh, locally sourced gredients, complemented by an extensive selection of wines, cocktails, and craft beers. The ceanfront setting adds an extra layer of charm to the dining experience, with breathtaking unset views that make every meal memorable.

or a more casual dining option, Lava's on Poipu Beach serves breakfast, lunch, and dinner in a id-back atmosphere. The menu features a variety of dishes, from hearty breakfast classics to esh seafood and tropical-inspired cocktails. Whether enjoying a leisurely meal with family or oping a drink by the pool, guests can savor the flavors of Kauai in every bite.

Sheraton Kauai Resort understands the importance of relaxation and recreation during a tropical getaway. The resort's oceanfront swimming pool provides a refreshing retreat for guests looking to unwind under the Hawaiian sun. The poolside area offers comfortable loungers and cabanas, creating an ideal spot to bask in the warmth and enjoy the tropical surroundings. For those seeking direct access to the beach, Poipu Beach is just steps away, inviting guests to indulge in the sun, surf, and sand.

In addition to water-based activities, the resort offers a range of recreational options to suit various interests. Fitness enthusiasts can maintain their workout routines at the resort's well-equipped fitness center, featuring state-of-the-art equipment and inspiring views. The on-site tennis courts provide an opportunity for guests to engage in friendly matches surrounded by the beauty of Kauai.

For those looking to rejuvenate mind and body, the Hawaiian Rainforest Spa at Sheraton Kauai Resort offers a tranquil haven. Inspired by traditional Hawaiian healing practices, the spa provides a variety of treatments, including massages, facials, and body scrubs. The skilled therapists use locally sourced ingredients to create a sensory experience that reflects the essence of the island's natural beauty.

Sheraton Kauai Resort is not only a haven for relaxation but also an ideal venue for events and special occasions. The resort features over 25,000 square feet of flexible indoor and outdoor meeting space, making it a popular choice for weddings, conferences, and other gatherings. The oceanfront lawn, with its breathtaking backdrop of the Pacific Ocean, offers a stunning setting for outdoor ceremonies and receptions.

Beyond the resort's borders, guests have easy access to some of Kauai's most iconic attraction The nearby Spouting Horn, a natural blowhole, showcases the island's geological wonders. The scenic beauty of Waimea Canyon, often referred to as the "Grand Canyon of the Pacific," is a short drive away, offering panoramic views of deep valleys and rugged cliffs. Adventurous soul can explore the famous Na Pali Coast by embarking on a boat tour or hiking the Kalalau Trail.

Sheraton Kauai Resort also places guests in proximity to cultural and historical sites. The Koloa Heritage Trail, just steps from the resort, takes visitors on a journey through the history of Kauai, with stops at ancient Hawaiian sites, sugar plantation remains, and historic churches. This immersive experience provides a deeper understanding of the island's rich heritage.

Sheraton Kauai Resort stands as a beacon of luxury and tranquility on the shores of Poipu Beach. Its commitment to providing guests with an authentic Hawaiian experience is evident in every detail, from the thoughtfully designed accommodations to the diverse dining options an recreational offerings. Whether seeking a romantic getaway, a family vacation, or a destinatio or a special event, Sheraton Kauai Resort offers a slice of paradise where the spirit of aloha thrives.

Hostels in Kauai: Affordable Accommodation in Paradise

auai, known for its stunning landscapes and outdoor adventures, offers a range of ccommodations for budget-conscious travelers. Hostels, in particular, provide an excellent ption for those looking to explore the island without breaking the bank. Here's a look at some opular hostels in Kauai along with their addresses:

1. **Kauai Beach House Hostel**

ddress: 4-1554 Kuhio Hwy, Kapaa, HI 96746

lestled on the eastern shore, Kauai Beach House Hostel offers a relaxed atmosphere and is vithin walking distance to the beach. The hostel provides dormitory-style rooms and private ccommodations.

2. **Kauai International Hostel**

ddress: 2439 Umi St, Lihue, HI 96766

entrally located in Lihue, this hostel is a great base for exploring the island. With a mix of hared and private rooms, Kauai International Hostel caters to various traveler preferences.

3. **Hanalei Hostel**

ddress: 5-5080 Kuhio Hwy, Hanalei, HI 96714

ituated in the charming town of Hanalei on the North Shore, this hostel provides a laid-back tmosphere with dormitory and private room options. It's conveniently close to popular ttractions like Hanalei Bay and Na Pali Coast.

4. **Kauai Palms Hotel**

ddress: 2931 Kalena St, Lihue, HI 96766

While not a traditional hostel, Kauai Palms Hotel offers budget-friendly accommodation with a range of room types. Located in Lihue, it provides easy access to the airport and other attractions.

5. Kauai YH Hostel

Address: 4530 Alawai Rd, Waimea, HI 96796

Part of the Hostelling International network, Kauai YH Hostel in Waimea offers affordable accommodation with a focus on community and sustainable travel. It's a short drive from Waimea Canyon.

Tips for Hostel Stays in Kauai:

1. Book in Advance:

Kauai is a popular destination, especially during peak seasons. To secure the best rates and availability, it's advisable to book your hostel stay well in advance.

2. Check Reviews:

Before making a reservation, read reviews from fellow travelers. Websites like Hostelworld and TripAdvisor provide insights into the experiences of previous guests.

3. Pack Essentials:

Hostel accommodations often include shared facilities. Be sure to pack essentials like a padlock flip-flops for shared showers, and a travel towel.

4. Explore Local Cuisine:

While hostels may offer kitchen facilities, take the opportunity to explore local restaurants and food trucks for a taste of Kauai's diverse cuisine.

5. Engage with Fellow Travelers:

Hostels foster a communal atmosphere. Take advantage of common areas and organized activities to meet fellow travelers and share experiences.

Kauai's hostels provide budget-friendly options for those seeking an authentic and affordable Hawaiian experience. Whether you're exploring the lush landscapes of Hanalei or the beaches of Kapaa, these hostels offer a convenient and economical way to enjoy the beauty of the Garden Isle.

Kauai Beach House Hostel: Embracing the Aloha Spirit

Kauai Beach House Hostel stands as a testament to the island's enchanting beauty and the welcoming spirit of Aloha. Offering budget-conscious travelers a unique and immersive experience, this hostel has become a popular choice for those seeking more than just a place to stay.

Conveniently situated at 4-1554 Kuhio Hwy, Kapaa, HI 96746, the Kauai Beach House Hostel boasts a prime location within walking distance to the beach. This strategic positioning allows guests easy access to the sun-kissed shores that Kauai is renowned for. The hostel's proximity to the ocean provides a soothing backdrop for those seeking a tranquil retreat.

The Kauai Beach House Hostel features a range of accommodations catering to various preferences and budgets. From dormitory-style rooms fostering a communal atmosphere to private rooms offering a more secluded experience, the hostel ensures that every guest finds a suitable space to call their own. The rooms are designed with simplicity and comfort in mind, allowing visitors to unwind after a day of exploration.

Beyond the cozy accommodations, the hostel's facilities and amenities contribute to its allure. The communal areas serve as vibrant hubs for social interaction, fostering a sense of community among travelers. Whether lounging in the common room, sharing stories in the kitchen, or enjoying the fresh air in the outdoor spaces, guests find ample opportunities to connect with like-minded individuals.

Kauai Beach House Hostel goes beyond being just a place to sleep; it's a gateway to Hawaiian culture. The hostel often organizes cultural events and activities, providing guests with a deeper understanding of the island's traditions. From lei-making workshops to hula dance lessons, these experiences add a layer of authenticity to the stay, allowing visitors to immerse themselves in the rich tapestry of Hawaiian heritage.

One of the highlights of staying at Kauai Beach House Hostel is the chance to savor local cuisine. The hostel's location in Kapaa means that guests are in close proximity to a variety of dining options. However, for those who prefer a culinary adventure within the hostel, communal kitchen facilities are available, encouraging guests to explore Hawaiian flavors and share meals with newfound friends.

Kauai is celebrated for its outdoor adventures, and the hostel capitalizes on its surroundings to provide guests with a range of activities. Whether it's organizing group hikes to nearby trails, arranging snorkeling excursions, or simply guiding guests to the best spots for sunset viewing, the hostel enhances the overall experience by connecting visitors with the natural wonders of the island.

In tune with the global shift towards sustainable travel, Kauai Beach House Hostel embraces eco-friendly practices. From recycling initiatives to energy conservation measures, the hostel strives to minimize its environmental impact. This commitment to sustainability aligns with the ethos of Kauai, a place where the beauty of nature is revered and protected.

What sets Kauai Beach House Hostel apart is its emphasis on community engagement. The hostel serves as a hub where travelers from different corners of the globe converge, creating a diverse and vibrant community. This interconnectedness is fostered through organized events, communal spaces, and a shared love for exploration.

The true measure of a hostel's success lies in the experiences of its guests. A glance at testimonials and reviews reveals a tapestry of positive encounters and cherished memories.

Visitors often praise the friendly staff, the welcoming atmosphere, and the hostel's role in creating lasting connections among travelers.

For those considering a visit to Kauai and a stay at the Beach House Hostel, it's advisable to plan ahead. The hostel's popularity means that reservations are often in high demand, particularly during peak seasons. Booking in advance ensures that you secure your spot in this haven of hospitality.

In the heart of Kauai's natural beauty, the Kauai Beach House Hostel stands as more than just a place to rest; it's a gateway to the soul of the island. Through its commitment to community, culture, and sustainability, the hostel encapsulates the essence of the Aloha Spirit. For those seeking an authentic and immersive experience on the Garden Isle, this hostel beckons with open arms, inviting travelers to embrace the magic of Kauai.

Kauai International Hostel: An Affordable Haven in Paradise

Kauai, the emerald gem of the Hawaiian archipelago, captivates visitors with its lush landscapes, pristine beaches, and vibrant culture. For budget-conscious travelers seeking an authentic Kauai experience, the Kauai International Hostel stands as a welcoming haven. Situated at 2439 Umi St, Lihue, HI 96766, this hostel embodies the spirit of aloha while providing affordable accommodation on the island.

Located in the heart of Lihue, Kauai International Hostel is strategically positioned for those looking to explore both the urban and natural wonders of the island. The hostel's proximity to the Lihue Airport makes it a convenient choice for travelers arriving by air. Its central location also allows easy access to Kauai's diverse attractions, from the bustling markets of Lihue to the scenic wonders of the Napali Coast.

Kauai International Hostel offers a range of accommodations to suit various preferences and budgets. The hostel's dormitory-style rooms provide an affordable option for solo travelers or those seeking a social atmosphere. With shared facilities and communal spaces, guests have the opportunity to connect with fellow travelers, sharing stories and forging friendships.

For those desiring more privacy, the hostel also offers private rooms. These provide a retreat for couples, families, or individuals seeking a quieter space while still enjoying the communal aspects of hostel living.

The atmosphere at Kauai International Hostel is warm and welcoming, creating a sense of home away from home. The common areas are designed for relaxation and socializing, featuring comfortable seating, communal kitchens, and outdoor spaces. Whether you're swapping travel tips with fellow guests or unwinding after a day of exploration, the hostel's communal spaces foster a sense of camaraderie among travelers from around the globe.

The hostel's staff, embodying the spirit of aloha, are often praised for their friendliness and helpfulness. They are a valuable resource for guests, offering local insights, recommendations for activities, and ensuring a smooth and enjoyable stay.

One of the key advantages of choosing Kauai International Hostel is its proximity to some of the island's most renowned attractions. Travelers can easily embark on day trips to the iconic Waimea Canyon, often referred to as the "Grand Canyon of the Pacific," or explore the lush landscapes of Wailua River State Park.

The hostel's central location also facilitates easy access to the vibrant cultural scene of Lihue. Guests can immerse themselves in the local markets, art galleries, and historical sites, gaining a deeper understanding of Kauai's rich heritage.

To ensure a comfortable and enjoyable stay at Kauai International Hostel, there are a few practical considerations to keep in mind. As with any hostel experience, guests are encouraged to bring essentials such as a padlock for securing personal items in shared dorms, flip-flops for communal showers, and a travel towel.

Booking in advance is advisable, especially during peak travel seasons when Kauai sees an influx of visitors. The hostel's popularity, coupled with its affordable rates, makes it a sought-after choice for those looking to experience the beauty of Kauai without breaking the bank.

While Kauai International Hostel provides communal kitchens for guests to prepare their meals, exploring the local culinary scene is a must. Kauai boasts a diverse array of dining options, from seaside seafood shacks to charming cafes serving up Hawaiian delicacies.

For those staying at the hostel, venturing into Lihue offers a chance to discover local eateries and savor the flavors of Kauai. From traditional poi to fresh poke bowls, the island's cuisine reflects its multicultural heritage and the abundance of fresh, locally sourced ingredients.

Kauai International Hostel not only serves as a gateway to the island's natural wonders but also provides opportunities for guests to engage with the local community. The hostel often organizes events and activities, allowing travelers to connect with the island's culture and traditions.

Guests may find themselves participating in a traditional lei-making workshop, learning hula dancing, or attending a local festival. These experiences not only enrich the travel journey but also foster a deeper connection to the spirit of Kauai.

In the realm of budget-friendly accommodations on the Garden Isle, Kauai International Hostel stands out as a gem. Its central location, welcoming atmosphere, and range of accommodation make it an ideal choice for travelers seeking affordability without compromising on the essence of their Kauai experience.

Whether you're a solo adventurer, a couple on a romantic getaway, or a family exploring the wonders of Kauai, the hostel provides a comfortable and community-driven space. As the sun sets over the Pacific and the sounds of the island embrace you, Kauai International Hostel becomes not just a place to rest but an integral part of the memories you'll carry from this enchanting Hawaiian paradise.

Hanalei Hostel

Hanalei Hostel stands as a haven for budget-conscious travelers seeking an authentic Hawaiian experience. With its laid-back atmosphere and proximity to some of the island's most iconic attractions, Hanalei Hostel has become a favored accommodation for those looking to immerse themselves in the beauty and charm of Hanalei.

The hostel, located at 5-5080 Kuhio Hwy, Hanalei, HI 96714, embodies the spirit of the local community while providing affordable lodging options for visitors. Its strategic location, just a stone's throw away from the renowned Hanalei Bay and the awe-inspiring Na Pali Coast, makes an ideal base for exploration.

Hanalei Hostel offers a range of accommodations to suit diverse traveler preferences. From shared dormitory-style rooms to private quarters, the hostel caters to solo adventurers, couples, and groups alike. The dormitories are well-appointed with comfortable bunk beds, storage lockers, and a communal atmosphere that encourages social interaction.

For those seeking more privacy, private rooms are available, offering a quiet retreat with the option to engage with fellow travelers in the common areas at their leisure. The rooms are tastefully decorated, capturing the essence of the island's vibrant culture.

The hostel's facilities are designed to enhance the overall guest experience. A communal kitchen allows travelers to prepare their meals, fostering a sense of community as individuals from different corners of the world come together to share stories and culinary creations. The kitchen is well-equipped, accommodating the diverse dietary needs of guests.

The common areas of the hostel provide spaces for relaxation and socialization. Whether lounging in the outdoor garden, enjoying the gentle Hawaiian breeze, or bonding over shared travel experiences in the cozy indoor lounge, guests find ample opportunities to connect with fellow adventurers.

What sets Hanalei Hostel apart is its commitment to facilitating authentic local experiences for its guests. The hostel often organizes guided excursions to nearby attractions, ensuring that visitors get the most out of their stay on the Garden Isle. From guided hikes through the lush landscapes of Hanalei to sunset beach picnics, these experiences contribute to a deeper understanding and appreciation of Kauai's natural beauty.

Hanalei Hostel is not just a place to stay; it's a community that values sustainability and responsible tourism. The hostel has implemented various eco-friendly practices, from recycling programs to energy-efficient initiatives. By choosing to stay at Hanalei Hostel, guests actively contribute to the preservation of Kauai's delicate ecosystem.

The staff at Hanalei Hostel, often comprised of knowledgeable locals, are eager to share inside tips and recommendations. Whether it's directing guests to hidden gems off the beaten path, suggesting the best spots for local cuisine, or providing insights into the island's rich cultural history, the hostel's team enhances the overall visitor experience.

Booking a stay at Hanalei Hostel is a straightforward process, with online reservations available. However, due to the hostel's popularity, especially during peak seasons, it is advisable to book well in advance to secure preferred dates and accommodation types.

For practical tips, guests are encouraged to pack essentials such as a padlock for lockers, comfortable footwear for exploring the island, and a reusable water bottle for eco-friendly adventures. The hostel's website and staff can provide additional guidance on what to bring for a comfortable and enjoyable stay.

Hanalei Hostel encapsulates the essence of Kauai's North Shore, offering more than just a place to rest for the night. It is a gateway to the island's natural wonders and a meeting point for like minded travelers. From its comfortable accommodations and communal spaces to its commitment to sustainable tourism, Hanalei Hostel provides an unparalleled opportunity to experience the beauty and hospitality of Kauai without breaking the bank. Whether you're a solo traveler on a tight budget or a group of friends seeking adventure, Hanalei Hostel welcomes you to embrace the aloha spirit and create lasting memories on the enchanting island of Kauai.

Kauai Palms Hotel

Kauai, the lush and picturesque island in Hawaii, is a haven for travelers seeking natural beauty and outdoor adventures. Amidst the stunning landscapes and vibrant culture, the choice of accommodation plays a crucial role in enhancing the overall experience. One such option that combines affordability with comfort is the Kauai Palms Hotel.

Situated at 2931 Kalena St, Lihue, HI 96766, Kauai Palms Hotel stands as a budget-friendly accommodation choice in the heart of Lihue. This establishment provides a relaxed and welcoming environment for visitors, making it an ideal base for exploring the diverse attractions that Kauai has to offer.

The Kauai Palms Hotel offers a range of room types to suit various preferences and travel needs. From standard rooms to larger suites, guests can choose accommodations that cater to both solo travelers and families. The rooms are designed with comfort in mind, featuring essential amenities to ensure a pleasant stay.

One of the key advantages of Kauai Palms Hotel is its central location in Lihue. Being the largest city on the island, Lihue serves as a convenient hub for exploring Kauai's attractions. The hotel's proximity to Lihue Airport is particularly beneficial for travelers looking to minimize travel time upon arrival.

The strategic location of Kauai Palms Hotel means that guests have easy access to a variety of attractions. Within a short drive, visitors can find themselves at Kalapaki Beach, known for its golden sands and gentle waves, making it an excellent spot for both relaxation and water activities.

For those interested in cultural experiences, the Grove Farm Homestead Museum and Kauai Museum are within reach, providing insights into the island's history and heritage. The hotel's central position also facilitates exploration of Nawiliwili Harbor, where visitors can embark on boat tours or enjoy waterfront dining.

Kauai Palms Hotel is equipped with facilities aimed at enhancing the overall guest experience. The outdoor pool provides a refreshing escape, allowing guests to unwind while surrounded by the tropical ambiance that characterizes Kauai. Additionally, the hotel offers free Wi-Fi, ensuring that guests can stay connected during their stay.

While Kauai Palms Hotel does not have an on-site restaurant, its central location means that guests have a plethora of dining options within walking or short driving distance. From local Hawaiian cuisine to international flavors, Lihue offers a diverse culinary scene that caters to various tastes and preferences.

What sets Kauai Palms Hotel apart is its integration into the local community. Staying at this hotel provides visitors with the opportunity to engage with the island's culture beyond its natural wonders. The friendly staff often serves as valuable resources, offering recommendations for hidden gems and lesser-known attractions that may not be featured in standard tourist guides.

Kauai Palms Hotel stands as a welcoming and budget-conscious choice for travelers exploring the enchanting island of Kauai. Its central location, comfortable accommodations, and integration into the local community make it a compelling option for those seeking an authentic Hawaiian experience without compromising on comfort. Whether you're a solo adventurer, a couple on a romantic getaway, or a family seeking a memorable vacation, Kauai Palms Hotel provides a convenient and affordable home base for your Kauai exploration.

Kauai YH Hostel: A Haven for Budget Travelers on the Garden Isle

Nestled in the heart of Waimea, Kauai YH Hostel stands as a welcoming haven for budget-conscious travelers seeking an authentic Hawaiian experience. As part of the renowned Hostelling International network, this hostel goes beyond being merely a place to rest; it's a community hub that embraces the spirit of sustainable travel.

The hostel, situated at 4530 Alawai Rd, Waimea, HI 96796, embodies the essence of Kauai's laid-back lifestyle. Its strategic location places guests within a short drive of Waimea Canyon, known as the "Grand Canyon of the Pacific," and offers convenient access to other local attractions.

From the moment guests step through the doors of Kauai YH Hostel, they are greeted by the warm and inviting atmosphere that characterizes the spirit of aloha. The hostel's staff, known for their friendliness and local insights, are eager to ensure that every visitor's stay is not just a series of nights but a memorable journey into the heart of Kauai.

The communal spaces within the hostel encourage interaction among guests. Whether it's swapping travel stories in the cozy lounge area or participating in organized activities, Kauai YH Hostel fosters a sense of community that resonates with the island's welcoming culture.

Kauai YH Hostel offers a range of accommodations to suit various preferences and budgets. Dormitory-style rooms provide an affordable option for solo travelers and those seeking to

connect with like-minded individuals. The hostel's commitment to sustainability is evident in its eco-friendly practices, making it a top choice for environmentally conscious travelers.

For those desiring more privacy, private rooms are available, allowing guests to unwind in their own space while still enjoying the vibrant atmosphere of the hostel. Clean and comfortable, the rooms are thoughtfully designed to provide a restful retreat after a day of exploration.

Waimea, the town that hosts Kauai YH Hostel, offers a glimpse into Kauai's rich history and natural beauty. Guests can stroll through the historic Waimea Town and immerse themselves in the local culture. The nearby Waimea Canyon, with its breathtaking views and hiking trails, is a must-visit for nature enthusiasts.

The hostel serves as a convenient starting point for exploring the island's diverse landscapes. Whether it's the lush greenery of the North Shore or the sun-kissed beaches of the South Shore, Kauai YH Hostel's central location allows guests to embark on memorable day trips to various parts of the island.

As a member of the Hostelling International network, Kauai YH Hostel is committed to sustainable tourism practices. From energy-efficient facilities to waste reduction initiatives, the hostel strives to minimize its environmental impact. Guests are encouraged to participate in eco-friendly initiatives, fostering a sense of responsibility for the beautiful surroundings they have the privilege to explore.

Community engagement is a cornerstone of Kauai YH Hostel's mission. The hostel collaborates with local businesses and artisans, ensuring that guests have opportunities to experience Kauai's unique culture firsthand. From guided tours led by knowledgeable locals to partnerships with nearby farmers' markets, the hostel actively contributes to the economic and cultural vitality of the Waimea community.

Kauai YH Hostel understands the importance of practical considerations for its guests. The hostel provides essential amenities, including a communal kitchen for self-catering, laundry facilities, and Wi-Fi connectivity. Additionally, the hostel staff is readily available to offer travel tips, assistance with booking activities, and recommendations for exploring Kauai like a seasoned local.

Kauai YH Hostel stands as more than just a place to stay; it is a gateway to the enchanting landscapes and vibrant culture of Kauai. From its commitment to sustainable practices to the warm hospitality that embodies the aloha spirit, the hostel creates an immersive experience for travelers seeking an authentic Hawaiian adventure. Whether embarking on solo journeys, connecting with fellow travelers, or engaging with the local community, guests at Kauai YH Hostel find themselves not just visitors but participants in the island's timeless narrative of beauty, community, and aloha.

SECTION 5: DINING AND CUISINE

Local Cuisine

Kauai, the lush and vibrant island in the Hawaiian archipelago, is not only renowned for its breathtaking landscapes but also for its rich and diverse local cuisine. As you traverse the island your taste buds embark on a journey of flavors influenced by the fusion of traditional Hawaiian, Asian, and Pacific Islander culinary traditions. In this gastronomic adventure, you'll discover the unique dishes and ingredients that define Kauai's local food culture.

At the heart of Kauai's cuisine is the emphasis on fresh, locally sourced ingredients. The island's fertile soil and favorable climate make it a haven for agriculture, providing a bountiful array of fruits, vegetables, and herbs. This commitment to freshness is evident in every dish, creating a dining experience that is not only delicious but also a celebration of the island's natural abundance.

Start your culinary exploration with the iconic Hawaiian dish, poke. A delectable marriage of raw fish, usually tuna, with soy sauce, sesame oil, green onions, and other flavorful additions, poke is a staple in Kauai's diet. The freshness of the fish is key, and many establishments pride themselves on sourcing the finest catch of the day.

As you venture further into the local food scene, you'll encounter plate lunches, a beloved tradition in Hawaii. These hearty meals typically consist of a protein, such as grilled chicken or kalua pork, accompanied by scoops of rice and macaroni salad. The simplicity of plate lunches belies their satisfying and comforting nature, making them a favorite among locals and visitors alike.

No exploration of Kauai's cuisine is complete without delving into the world of traditional Hawaiian luau. This festive feast is a true sensory experience, featuring an array of dishes that showcase the island's agricultural prowess. Immerse yourself in the flavors of kalua pig, slow-cooked in an underground oven, or laulau, a dish where pork and sometimes fish are wrapped in taro leaves and steamed to perfection.

For those with a sweet tooth, Kauai offers a delightful array of treats, with one standout being haupia. This coconut milk-based dessert is both creamy and refreshing, providing a perfect conclusion to any meal. Equally tempting are malasadas, Portuguese-inspired doughnuts that have become a beloved local delicacy. Whether dusted with sugar or filled with tropical fruit jams, malasadas are a decadent indulgence.

As you traverse the diverse regions of Kauai, you'll encounter specialties unique to each area. In Hanalei, for instance, don't miss the chance to savor taro burgers or indulge in a shave ice, a refreshing concoction of finely shaved ice topped with an array of tropical syrups. On the south shore, fresh seafood takes center stage, with fish tacos and coconut shrimp becoming must-try dishes.

Kauai's culinary landscape is also shaped by the cultural influences of its diverse population. Japanese, Filipino, and Chinese communities have left an indelible mark on the island's food scene, contributing dishes like saimin, a noodle soup, and manapua, a Hawaiian take on the Chinese bao. These culinary fusions reflect the dynamic and harmonious coexistence of cultures on the island.

In addition to exploring local eateries, consider attending one of Kauai's farmers' markets. Here, you can engage with local farmers and artisans, gaining insight into the island's agricultural practices and discovering unique products like lilikoi (passion fruit) butter and honey infused with the essence of tropical flowers.

Kauai's local cuisine is a vibrant tapestry of flavors, colors, and textures that reflects the island's natural beauty and cultural diversity. Whether you're savoring the simplicity of poke by the ocean or indulging in a festive luau under the stars, every bite tells a story of the land, the sea, and the people who call this enchanting island home.

Kauai Culinary Delights: A Gastronomic Journey

1. **Merriman's Fish House**

Address: 2829 Ala Kalanikaumaka St, Poipu, HI 96756

A culinary gem nestled in Poipu, Merriman's Fish House is renowned for its farm-to-table concept. Chef Peter Merriman showcases the island's freshest ingredients in dishes like the Opakapaka (Hawaiian pink snapper) and the decadent Kauai Shrimp Risotto.

2. **The Beach House Restaurant**

Address: 5022 Lawai Rd, Koloa, HI 96756

Perched on the edge of Lawai Beach, The Beach House Restaurant offers a stunning oceanfront dining experience. Specializing in Pacific Rim cuisine, this restaurant boasts a diverse menu with highlights such as the Ahi Tuna Poke and the Macadamia Nut-Encrusted Mahi-Mahi.

3. **Bar Acuda**

Address: 5-5161 Kuhio Hwy, Hanalei, HI 96714

Tucked away in the charming town of Hanalei, Bar Acuda is a tapas-style restaurant serving up Mediterranean-inspired small plates. The intimate setting and carefully crafted menu make it a favorite among locals and visitors alike.

4. Duke's Kauai

Address: 3610 Rice St, Lihue, HI 96766

Named after the legendary Duke Kahanamoku, this waterfront restaurant in Lihue pays homage to Hawaiian beach boy culture. Duke's Kauai features a diverse menu with Hawaiian-inspired dishes like Huli Huli Chicken and Kauai Prawn & Clams Linguine.

5. Eating House 1849

Address: 2330 Hoone Rd, Koloa, HI 96756

Helmed by renowned chef Roy Yamaguchi, Eating House 1849 blends traditional Hawaiian flavors with global culinary techniques. The menu showcases dishes like the Miso-Yaki Butterfish and the flavorful Plantation Paella.

6. Oasis on the Beach

Address: 4-820 Kuhio Hwy, Kapaa, HI 96746

Located in Kapaa, Oasis on the Beach offers a delightful oceanfront dining experience. The menu features locally sourced ingredients, with highlights including the Ahi Bruschetta and the Kalua Pork Wontons.

7. Red Salt

Address: 2251 Poipu Rd, Koloa, HI 96756

Situated in the Ko'a Kea Hotel & Resort, Red Salt is a culinary haven led by Executive Chef Noelani Planas. The menu reflects a fusion of Hawaiian and global influences, with signature dishes like the Red Salt Poke and the Kurobuta Pork Chop.

8. Postcards Café

Address: 5-5075 Kuhio Hwy, Hanalei, HI 96714

Housed in a plantation-era cottage in Hanalei, Postcards Café offers a farm-to-table dining experience. The menu, which changes daily, features organic and locally sourced ingredients, with standout dishes such as the Ahi Tartare and the Lilikoi Crème Brulee.

9. JO2 Natural Cuisine

Address: 4-971 Kuhio Hwy, Kapaa, HI 96746

Known for its commitment to natural and sustainable cuisine, JO2 offers a diverse menu with options for all tastes, from the Lobster & Kauai Shrimp Ravioli to the Braised Short Rib. The restaurant's cozy atmosphere adds to the overall dining experience.

10. Kauai Grill

Address: 5520 Ka Haku Rd, Princeville, HI 96722

Nestled in the St. Regis Princeville Resort, Kauai Grill is a culinary masterpiece by acclaimed chef Jean-Georges Vongerichten. The menu boasts a selection of prime steaks, fresh seafood, and inventive appetizers, all set against breathtaking views of Hanalei Bay.

Merriman's Fish House

Merriman's Fish House, a culinary beacon nestled in the heart of Poipu, Kauai, stands as a testament to the island's rich culinary heritage and commitment to farm-to-table excellence. From its unassuming location at 2829 Ala Kalanikaumaka Street, this restaurant has become a gastronomic haven, drawing locals and visitors alike into its embrace.

Chef Peter Merriman, a pioneer of Hawaii's regional cuisine movement, established Merriman's Fish House with a vision to celebrate the freshest local ingredients while showcasing the unique flavors of the Hawaiian Islands. As you step through the doors of Merriman's, you are welcomed into a world where the bounty of Kauai's land and sea converges to create a dining experience unlike any other.

The ambiance at Merriman's Fish House is a harmonious blend of casual elegance and island charm. The restaurant's interior reflects the laid-back spirit of Kauai, with warm hues, wooden accents, and panoramic windows that offer glimpses of the lush surroundings. Whether you're seated indoors or on the open-air lanai, the atmosphere sets the stage for a memorable culinary journey.

The menu at Merriman's is a showcase of the island's natural abundance, with a focus on locally sourced ingredients that capture the essence of Kauai. As a fish house, the restaurant takes pride in its seafood offerings, featuring daily catches that are a testament to the island's rich marine life. The Opakapaka, a Hawaiian pink snapper, is a highlight, prepared with meticulous attention to detail to preserve its delicate flavor and texture.

One of the signature dishes at Merriman's is the Kauai Shrimp Risotto. This delectable creation exemplifies Chef Peter Merriman's commitment to blending global culinary techniques with local ingredients. The succulent Kauai shrimp, plump and flavorful, are expertly paired with creamy risotto, creating a symphony of textures and tastes that dance on the palate.

Beyond the seafood offerings, Merriman's Fish House embraces the farm-to-table concept with an array of dishes that highlight the island's vibrant produce. From crisp, locally grown greens to the sweetest tropical fruits, each ingredient is selected with care to ensure a dining experience that reflects the true flavors of Kauai. The menu evolves with the seasons, allowing guests to savor the freshest offerings throughout the year.

The commitment to sustainability is a core philosophy at Merriman's Fish House. Chef Merriman's dedication to supporting local farmers, fishermen, and ranchers not only contributes to the restaurant's exceptional cuisine but also fosters a sense of community. This ethos is reflected not only in the ingredients sourced but also in the efforts to minimize the restaurant's environmental impact, making Merriman's a pioneer in responsible dining.

The culinary expertise at Merriman's extends beyond the kitchen, as the restaurant boasts an impressive selection of wines and craft cocktails. The wine list is carefully curated to complement the diverse flavors of the menu, with options ranging from crisp Sauvignon Blancs to robust Cabernet Sauvignons. The skilled mixologists behind the bar craft cocktails that showcase tropical ingredients, providing the perfect prelude or accompaniment to a memorable meal.

Service at Merriman's Fish House is characterized by warm hospitality and a genuine passion for sharing the island's culinary treasures. The staff, well-versed in the intricacies of the menu, is adept at guiding diners through the culinary journey, offering insights into the origins of each dish and the farmers and fishermen who contribute to its creation.

For those seeking a more intimate dining experience, Merriman's offers private dining options that elevate any special occasion. Whether it's a romantic dinner for two, a family celebration,

or a corporate gathering, the restaurant's commitment to excellence extends to every aspect of the dining experience.

Merriman's Fish House is not just a restaurant; it's a celebration of Kauai's bounty, a testament to Chef Peter Merriman's culinary vision, and a gathering place for those who appreciate the art of dining. As you savor each bite, you embark on a journey through the flavors of Kauai, where the land and sea come together to create a symphony of tastes that linger in memory long after the meal is over. In every dish, Merriman's Fish House captures the essence of Kauai, making it culinary destination that transcends the ordinary and invites guests to savor the extraordinary.

The Beach House Restaurant

The Beach House Restaurant, located at 5022 Lawai Rd, Koloa, HI 96756, stands as an iconic culinary destination on the picturesque island of Kauai. Nestled on the edge of Lawai Beach, this dining establishment not only offers a feast for the palate but also treats guests to breathtaking oceanfront views. Known for its Pacific Rim cuisine and commitment to using fresh, locally sourced ingredients, The Beach House has earned a stellar reputation among locals and tourists alike.

The restaurant's prime location sets the stage for a dining experience that goes beyond the plate. The exterior's plantation-style architecture blends seamlessly with the tropical surroundings, creating an inviting ambiance that captures the essence of Kauai's laid-back elegance. As one approaches The Beach House, the rhythmic sound of crashing waves and the scent of saltwater create an atmosphere that transports diners to a world where culinary excellence meets the beauty of nature.

Upon entering The Beach House, guests are welcomed by a warm and inviting interior that reflects the island's charm. The décor, characterized by muted tones and natural materials, complements the stunning backdrop of the ocean visible through expansive windows. The restaurant's design not only enhances the dining experience but also pays homage to Kauai's rich cultural and environmental heritage.

The menu at The Beach House is a testament to the culinary expertise of the chefs, who artfully blend flavors inspired by the Pacific Rim. With a commitment to showcasing the best of local produce, the dishes celebrate the diversity of Kauai's bounty. One standout feature is the restaurant's dedication to sustainability, reflected in the use of fresh, seasonal ingredients sourced from local farmers, fishermen, and ranchers.

Seafood takes center stage on the menu, with an array of dishes that highlight the island's abundance of marine delicacies. The Ahi Tuna Poke, a Hawaiian classic, is a popular starter that combines the freshest tuna with traditional seasonings, offering a burst of flavors that sets the tone for the meal. Another seafood delight is the Macadamia Nut-Encrusted Mahi-Mahi, a signature dish that showcases the fusion of local ingredients with international culinary techniques.

While seafood is a highlight, The Beach House caters to a variety of tastes with its diverse menu. The culinary team has crafted options that include vegetarian and meat-based dishes, ensuring that every diner finds something to delight their taste buds. The Coconut-Crusted Lamb Chops and the Tropical Fruit Salad with local greens exemplify the restaurant's commitment to catering to different preferences while maintaining a high standard of culinary excellence.

Complementing the delectable dishes is an extensive wine list that features both local and international selections. The Beach House offers a curated collection of wines that enhances the dining experience, with knowledgeable staff on hand to provide recommendations for perfect pairings. Whether enjoying a romantic evening or a family gathering, the restaurant's commitment to delivering a memorable dining experience extends to its beverage offerings.

In addition to its regular menu, The Beach House offers seasonal specials that showcase the creativity of the culinary team. These specials often highlight unique, limited-time ingredients, providing returning patrons with fresh culinary experiences during each visit. The restaurant's dedication to innovation and variety ensures that it remains a dynamic force in Kauai's ever-evolving culinary landscape.

Service at The Beach House is as exceptional as its cuisine. The attentive and knowledgeable staff contributes to the overall ambiance, creating an atmosphere where guests feel welcomed and cared for. From the moment patrons step through the door until the last bite is savored, the staff's dedication to providing top-notch hospitality enhances the dining experience.

The Beach House isn't just a place to enjoy a meal; it's a venue for special occasions and memorable moments. The restaurant's oceanfront lawn serves as an idyllic setting for weddings and events, with the sound of waves providing a natural soundtrack to celebrations. The dedicated events team works closely with guests to ensure that every detail, from the menu to the décor, aligns with the vision for their special day.

As the sun sets over Lawai Beach, The Beach House undergoes a transformation, transitioning from a vibrant daytime eatery to a romantic evening escape. The twilight hours bring a sense of enchantment to the restaurant, and diners can witness the mesmerizing dance of colors on the ocean as they savor their meals. The Beach House has become synonymous with sunset dining on Kauai, offering an unparalleled view of the sun dipping below the horizon.

The Beach House Restaurant on Kauai stands as more than a culinary destination; it is a sensory experience that celebrates the island's natural beauty and rich flavors. From the carefully curated menu to the oceanfront setting, every aspect of the restaurant has been designed to immerse diners in the essence of Kauai. For those seeking a gastronomic journey that transcends the ordinary, The Beach House remains a beacon of culinary excellence on the Garden Isle.

Bar Acuda

Bar Acuda, a culinary haven nestled in the heart of Hanalei, Kauai, beckons food enthusiasts with its enchanting ambiance and a menu that seamlessly blends Mediterranean flavors with locally-sourced ingredients. This dining establishment, located at 5-5161 Kuhio Hwy, Hanalei, HI 96714, has established itself as a go-to destination for those seeking an intimate and memorable gastronomic experience on the island.

As patrons step into Bar Acuda, they are greeted by an inviting atmosphere that effortlessly combines rustic charm with contemporary design. The restaurant's interior exudes warmth, featuring wooden accents, soft lighting, and an open layout that fosters a sense of community among diners. The carefully curated playlist adds a melodic backdrop to the dining experience, enhancing the overall ambiance.

One of the defining features of Bar Acuda is its commitment to the tapas-style dining experience. The menu, a testament to the culinary prowess of the chefs, offers an array of small plates that showcase the diverse and vibrant flavors of Mediterranean cuisine. Each dish is a masterpiece, reflecting a meticulous attention to detail and a dedication to using the freshest local ingredients.

One cannot explore the offerings at Bar Acuda without delving into the starters. The Charcuterie Board, a mosaic of cured meats, artisanal cheeses, and house-made pickles, sets the tone for the meal, inviting diners to savor the rich and varied tastes that lie ahead. The Grilled Octopus, a signature dish, exemplifies the chef's mastery in bringing out the natural essence of ingredients, leaving patrons with a symphony of flavors on their palates.

Moving on to the main course, Bar Acuda continues to impress with its selection of seafood, meat, and vegetarian options. The Kauai Shrimp Risotto, a perennial favorite, exemplifies the fusion of local and Mediterranean influences, with plump shrimp perfectly complementing the creamy Arborio rice. For those seeking a carnivorous delight, the Lamb Chops with Mint Pesto deliver a succulent and flavorful experience, showcasing the restaurant's commitment to quality cuts and innovative pairings.

The commitment to locally-sourced ingredients is not only evident in the food but extends to the thoughtfully crafted cocktail menu. Bar Acuda's mixologists expertly blend fresh fruits, herbs, and spirits to create concoctions that mirror the island's vibrant spirit. The Hanalei Mule featuring Kauai-made ginger beer, pays homage to the restaurant's locale, while the Lilikoi Martini adds a tropical twist to the classic cocktail.

The dessert menu at Bar Acuda Is a sweet conclusion to the culinary journey. The Chocolate Budino, a decadent chocolate pudding, satisfies the most discerning sweet tooth, while the Tropical Fruit Sorbet offers a refreshing and palate-cleansing option for those seeking a lighter ending to their meal.

Beyond the exquisite menu, the staff at Bar Acuda plays a pivotal role in elevating the overall dining experience. The waitstaff, well-versed in the intricacies of the menu, provide attentive and personalized service, ensuring that patrons feel not just like customers but valued guests. The chefs, hidden maestros in the kitchen, bring a passion for culinary innovation to each dish, creating a symphony of flavors that resonates with every bite.

The success of Bar Acuda is not solely attributed to its delectable menu and inviting ambiance; it is also deeply rooted in its connection to the local community. The restaurant actively collaborates with nearby farmers, fishermen, and artisans to source the freshest produce and ingredients. This commitment to supporting local businesses not only enhances the quality of the dishes but also contributes to the sustainability and resilience of the island's food ecosystem.

As day turns to night, the outdoor seating at Bar Acuda comes alive with a charming ambiance under the starlit Hawaiian sky. The gentle rustling of palm trees and the distant sound of the ocean provide a serene backdrop, creating an enchanting atmosphere for patrons to unwind and revel in the culinary delights that unfold before them.

Bar Acuda stands as a culinary gem in Hanalei, Kauai, offering a transcendent dining experience that marries Mediterranean influences with the rich tapestry of Hawaiian flavors. From the first sip of a craft cocktail to the last bite of a sumptuous dessert, patrons embark on a gastronomic journey that celebrates the artistry of food and the spirit of community. For those seeking a memorable dining experience in Kauai, Bar Acuda remains an iconic destination, inviting guests to savor the essence of the island through its exceptional cuisine.

Duke's Kauai

In the heart of Kauai, nestled along the picturesque coastline of Lihue, lies a culinary gem that pays homage to the legendary Duke Kahanamoku. Duke's Kauai, an iconic waterfront restaurant, seamlessly blends the rich cultural heritage of Hawaii with a contemporary dining experience. From its breathtaking ocean views to its delectable menu, Duke's Kauai is a celebration of Hawaiian beach boy culture and a testament to the island's culinary excellence.

Duke's Kauai, located at 3610 Rice St, Lihue, HI 96766, is more than just a dining establishment; it's an immersive experience that captures the spirit of Aloha. Named after Duke Kahanamoku, a pioneering surfer, Olympic swimmer, and the "Father of Modern Surfing," the restaurant embodies his legacy and the laid-back, welcoming atmosphere that he was known for.

As patrons step into Duke's Kauai, they are greeted by a warm and inviting ambiance that reflects the essence of Duke's own hospitality. The interior is adorned with memorabilia honoring Duke Kahanamoku's achievements, including vintage surfboards, photographs, and mementos from his illustrious career. The décor sets the stage for a dining experience that seamlessly weaves together the past and present, inviting guests to connect with the rich history of Hawaiian surfing culture.

One of the standout features of Duke's Kauai is its unparalleled oceanfront location. The restaurant is strategically positioned to offer breathtaking views of the Pacific Ocean, providing diners with a front-row seat to the natural beauty that defines Kauai. Whether seated indoors or on the expansive outdoor lanai, patrons are treated to panoramic vistas of the sparkling blue waters, with the sound of gentle waves providing a soothing soundtrack to their dining experience.

The outdoor seating area, surrounded by lush tropical landscaping, creates an oasis-like setting that enhances the overall ambiance. As the sun sets over the horizon, Duke's Kauai transforms into a romantic haven, with the changing colors of the sky mirrored in the ocean below. It's a prime spot for couples seeking a memorable evening or families looking to enjoy a sunset dinner in a captivating environment.

Culinary Excellence with a Hawaiian Twist

Duke's Kauai takes pride in its commitment to showcasing the flavors of Hawaii through a diverse and thoughtfully crafted menu. Executive Chef, [Chef's Name], leads the culinary team in

curating a selection of dishes that highlight the island's bountiful seafood, locally sourced produce, and unique culinary traditions.

Appetizers and Starters:

The culinary journey at Duke's Kauai often begins with an array of tempting appetizers. The Ah Poke Stacks, featuring fresh Hawaiian ahi tuna, avocado, and crispy wontons, offer a refreshing start. The Coconut Shrimp, served with a zesty lilikoi chili sauce, provides a delightful balance o flavors, embodying the tropical essence of Kauai.

Signature Entrees:

The entrée selection at Duke's Kauai is a testament to the restaurant's commitment to culinary excellence. The Huli Huli Chicken, a Hawaiian-style rotisserie chicken glazed with a pineapple-soy marinade, is a local favorite that captures the essence of traditional island barbecue. For seafood enthusiasts, the Kauai Prawn & Clams Linguine, featuring succulent prawns and local clams in a garlic white wine sauce, is a must-try, showcasing the abundance of fresh seafood available in the region.

Steaks and Ribs:

Duke's Kauai also caters to those with a penchant for hearty steaks and ribs. The Grilled Filet Mignon, cooked to perfection and served with a truffle mushroom demi-glace, is a carnivore's delight. The Baby Back Ribs, slow-cooked and slathered in Duke's barbecue sauce, exemplify the restaurant's commitment to bold and flavorful dishes.

Fresh Catch of the Day:

One of the highlights of dining at Duke's Kauai is the Fresh Catch of the Day. Featuring locally sourced fish, often caught by fishermen from the nearby waters, this dish allows patrons to savor the true essence of Hawaiian seafood. The preparation varies daily, showcasing the versatility and creativity of the culinary team.

Duke's Beachside Burger:

For those craving a classic American dish with a tropical twist, the Duke's Beachside Burger is a popular choice. This hearty burger, topped with bacon, cheddar cheese, avocado, and a special sauce, is a satisfying option for those looking to indulge in a taste of paradise.

Desserts that Delight:

No culinary journey is complete without a sweet finale, and Duke's Kauai delivers with a tempting selection of desserts. The Hula Pie, a signature creation featuring macadamia nut ice cream, chocolate cookie crust, hot fudge, and whipped cream, has become a legendary favorite among both locals and visitors. The Lilikoi Cheesecake, showcasing the tropical flavors of passion fruit, provides a fitting end to a memorable meal.

Libations and Libations

Complementing the delectable menu at Duke's Kauai is an extensive selection of libations that adds an extra layer of enjoyment to the dining experience. The restaurant's skilled mixologists craft an array of signature cocktails, incorporating tropical fruits, premium spirits, and innovative combinations that pay homage to the Hawaiian culture.

Duke's Mai Tai:

No visit to Duke's Kauai is complete without sipping on the iconic Duke's Mai Tai. This classic cocktail, featuring a blend of premium rums, fresh lime juice, orange liqueur, and orgeat syrup, is a refreshing and flavorful ode to the tropical paradise that surrounds the restaurant.

Tropical Cocktails:

In addition to the Mai Tai, Duke's Kauai offers a variety of tropical cocktails that capture the spirit of the islands. The POG Punch, a blend of passion fruit, orange, and guava juices with a hint of rum, is a fruity concoction that transports patrons to the shores of Hawaii with every sip.

Extensive Wine List:

For wine enthusiasts, Duke's Kauai boasts an extensive wine list that complements the diverse flavors of the menu. From crisp Sauvignon Blancs to full-bodied Cabernet Sauvignons, the curated selection offers options for every palate.

Local Craft Beers:

To celebrate the vibrant craft beer scene in Hawaii, Duke's Kauai also features a rotating selection of local brews. Patrons can enjoy a cold pint of a refreshing island beer, providing a perfect accompaniment to the laid-back atmosphere of the restaurant.

Duke's Kauai not only satisfies the palate but also delights the senses with live music and entertainment. Throughout the week, talented local musicians take the stage, serenading diners with a mix of traditional Hawaiian melodies, contemporary hits, and laid-back tunes that enhance the overall dining experience. The rhythmic sounds of ukuleles and guitars create a lively and festive atmosphere, inviting patrons to immerse themselves in the cultural richness of Kauai.

A visit to Duke's Kauai is not just about the food and ambiance; it's about the genuine hospitality that defines the Hawaiian spirit. The staff at Duke's Kauai goes above and beyond to ensure that every guest feels welcomed and cared for. From the moment patrons step through the door to the final farewell, the attentive and friendly service adds an extra layer of warmth to the overall dining experience.

Duke's Kauai stands as a testament to the enduring legacy of Duke Kahanamoku and the vibrant culinary scene of Kauai. Whether seeking a romantic dinner with a view, a family-friendly atmosphere, or a taste of authentic Hawaiian flavors, Duke's Kauai delivers on every front. From the oceanfront elegance to the delectable menu and live entertainment, the restaurant offers a comprehensive and immersive experience that captures the essence of Kauai's Aloha spirit.

As patrons indulge in the culinary creations, sip on tropical cocktails, and soak in the stunning views, they become part of a tradition that spans generations. Duke's Kauai is not just a restaurant; it's a destination where memories are made, and the spirit of Duke Kahanamoku lives on, inviting all to embrace the beauty of Kauai and the joy of sharing good food and good times with loved ones.

n the heart of Lihue, Duke's Kauai stands as a beacon of culinary excellence, a tribute to the past, and a celebration of the vibrant present that defines this enchanting island in the Pacific.

ating House 1849

ating House 1849, a culinary treasure situated at 2330 Hoone Rd, Koloa, HI 96756, stands as a estament to the fusion of traditional Hawaiian flavors and global culinary techniques. Founded y the renowned chef Roy Yamaguchi, Eating House 1849 is a celebration of Hawaii's rich ulinary heritage, drawing inspiration from the island's plantation era and infusing it with a nodern, innovative twist.

he restaurant, named after one of the first restaurants in Hawaii opened by a Portuguese usinessman in the mid-1800s, pays homage to the diverse cultural influences that have shaped lawaiian cuisine over the years. As you step into Eating House 1849, you are welcomed by a varm and inviting atmosphere that perfectly complements the culinary delights that await vithin.

he menu at Eating House 1849 is a carefully curated symphony of flavors, featuring dishes that howcase the bounty of Hawaii's local produce and seafood. One of the standout dishes that as captured the hearts and palates of diners is the Miso-Yaki Butterfish. This signature dish erfectly encapsulates the essence of Eating House 1849's approach to cuisine – a harmonious lend of traditional Hawaiian ingredients with contemporary culinary techniques.

he Miso-Yaki Butterfish, a culinary masterpiece in its own right, features succulent butterfish narinated in a miso glaze that imparts a rich umami flavor. The dish is then expertly grilled to erfection, resulting in a melt-in-your-mouth experience that is both satisfying and nforgettable. This dish, like many others on the menu, reflects Chef Roy Yamaguchi's ommitment to using the freshest local ingredients to create a dining experience that is niquely Hawaiian.

Beyond the Miso-Yaki Butterfish, the menu at Eating House 1849 boasts a diverse array of ppetizers, entrees, and desserts that cater to a variety of tastes. Whether you're a seafood enthusiast, a lover of grilled meats, or a vegetarian seeking innovative plant-based options, ating House 1849 has something to tantalize your taste buds.

or those seeking a taste of Hawaii's culinary history, the Plantation Paella is a must-try. This nearty and flavorful dish pays homage to the multicultural plantation era, featuring a tantalizing nix of local seafood, Portuguese sausage, and saffron-infused rice. Each bite tells a story of the diverse influences that have shaped Hawaiian cuisine, making it a culinary journey through time.

In addition to the delectable entrees, Eating House 1849 offers an array of appetizers that serve as a perfect prelude to the main course. The Ahi Poke Stack, a visually stunning dish, showcases the freshness of Hawaii's renowned ahi tuna. Layers of marinated ahi are stacked with avocado and crispy wontons, creating a dish that is as pleasing to the eyes as it is to the palate.

No culinary adventure is complete without indulging in a sweet finale, and Eating House 1849 delivers on this front with a selection of mouthwatering desserts. The Lilikoi Crème Brulee, a twist on the classic French dessert, features a luscious passion fruit custard with a perfectly caramelized sugar crust. It's a delightful way to round off a meal, leaving a lingering sweetness that stays with you long after you've left the restaurant.

Eating House 1849 goes beyond being a mere dining establishment; it is a cultural experience that immerses patrons in the rich tapestry of Hawaii's culinary heritage. The restaurant's commitment to using locally sourced, sustainable ingredients not only ensures a fresh and flavorful dining experience but also aligns with the growing movement towards responsible and conscious dining.

The ambiance of Eating House 1849 adds to the overall dining experience. The restaurant's décor seamlessly blends modern aesthetics with nods to the plantation era, creating a space that feels both contemporary and steeped in history. The open kitchen concept allows diners to witness the culinary artistry happening in real-time, adding an interactive element to the dining experience.

Chef Roy Yamaguchi's influence is palpable in every aspect of Eating House 1849. With a culinary career that spans decades and has earned him acclaim worldwide, Chef Roy brings a level of expertise and passion to the restaurant that elevates it to a league of its own. His commitment to showcasing the best of Hawaiian cuisine while pushing culinary boundaries has made Eating House 1849 a destination for food enthusiasts seeking a truly memorable dining experience.

Beyond the gastronomic delights, Eating House 1849 actively engages with the local community, supporting farmers, fishermen, and artisans. This commitment to sustainability and community involvement adds an extra layer of depth to the dining experience, allowing patrons to feel a connection not only to the food on their plates but also to the broader cultural and environmental context of Hawaii.

As you savor each bite at Eating House 1849, you can't help but appreciate the meticulous attention to detail that goes into every dish. The menu, a carefully crafted symphony of flavors and textures, reflects Chef Roy Yamaguchi's dedication to culinary excellence. Each ingredient is houghtfully selected, and each dish is a masterpiece that tells a story of Hawaii's culinary volution.

ating House 1849 stands as a culinary beacon in Kauai, inviting diners on a journey through the lavors of Hawaii's past and present. From the moment you enter the restaurant to the last bite f dessert, the experience is a celebration of the island's rich cultural heritage and the vibrant

apestry of flavors that define Hawaiian cuisine. Eating House 1849 is not just a restaurant; it is destination for those seeking an immersive and unforgettable dining experience in the heart f Koloa.

Oasis on the Beach: A Culinary Haven in Kapaa, Kauai

Iestled along the eastern shore of Kauai, the Garden Isle of Hawaii, lies a culinary oasis that aptivates the senses and invites patrons on a gastronomic journey like no other. Oasis on the each, situated at 4-820 Kuhio Hwy, Kapaa, HI 96746, stands as a testament to the vibrant and iverse culinary landscape of Kauai, offering a delightful blend of locally sourced ingredients, reative flavors, and breathtaking oceanfront views.

Jpon entering Oasis on the Beach, guests are greeted by a warm and inviting ambiance. The estaurant's open-air design allows the gentle Hawaiian breeze to sweep through, creating a elaxed and comfortable atmosphere. The interior, adorned with subtle tropical décor, mirrors he laid-back charm of the surrounding environment.

he focal point of the dining experience at Oasis on the Beach is undoubtedly the panoramic cean views. The restaurant's prime location, just steps away from the sandy shores, provides iners with a front-row seat to the mesmerizing beauty of the Pacific. Whether seated inside or n the outdoor lanai, patrons can savor their meals against the backdrop of the azure sea and he rhythmic sounds of the waves.

ed by Executive Chef Nyel Drury, Oasis on the Beach takes pride in its commitment to howcasing the rich culinary heritage of Kauai. The menu is a symphony of flavors, skillfully lending traditional Hawaiian ingredients with global influences. Each dish is a work of art, a estament to the chef's dedication to sourcing the freshest local produce and seafood.

egin your culinary journey with the Ahi Bruschetta, a delightful fusion of fresh ahi poke, vocado, and a zesty tomato relish served on crisp crostinis. The Kalua Pork Wontons are a avory sensation, featuring slow-cooked pulled pork encased in delicate wonton wrappers, ccompanied by a tangy hoisin dipping sauce.

For the main course, indulge in the Macadamia Nut Mahi-Mahi, a signature dish that showcase the delicate flavors of locally caught mahi-mahi paired with a macadamia nut crust, providing a delightful crunch. The Coconut Seafood Curry is a fragrant and flavorful option, featuring a medley of island fish, shrimp, and scallops bathed in a rich coconut curry sauce.

No culinary journey is complete without a sweet ending. Oasis on the Beach's dessert menu offers a tempting array of treats, including the Lilikoi (passion fruit) Crème Brulee, a velvety custard with a perfectly caramelized sugar crust, and the Chocolate Decadence, a rich flourless chocolate cake served with vanilla bean ice cream.

Beyond its culinary excellence, Oasis on the Beach is dedicated to sustainable and responsible dining practices. The restaurant partners with local farmers and fishermen to ensure the freshest and most ethically sourced ingredients. By embracing the farm-to-table concept, Oasis on the Beach not only supports the local community but also minimizes its environmental footprint.

The outdoor seating area at Oasis on the Beach provides an unparalleled dining experience. As the sun dips below the horizon, casting hues of orange and pink across the sky, patrons can revel in the romantic ambiance created by softly glowing tiki torches. The rhythmic ebb and flow of the tide become the soundtrack to a memorable evening, making Oasis on the Beach an ideal spot for romantic dinners and special celebrations.

What sets Oasis on the Beach apart extends beyond its culinary prowess and breathtaking views. The restaurant embodies the spirit of aloha, a genuine and heartfelt expression of love, compassion, and harmony. The staff, attentive and friendly, ensures that every guest feels not just welcomed but embraced by the warm embrace of Hawaiian hospitality.

Practical Information

Address: 4-820 Kuhio Hwy, Kapaa, HI 96746

Phone: (808) 822-9332

Website: Oasis on the Beach

Hours of Operation:

Lunch: Monday to Saturday, 11:00 AM to 3:00 PM

Dinner: Daily, 5:30 PM to 9:00 PM

Oasis on the Beach in Kapaa, Kauai, transcends the boundaries of a typical dining experience. It is a culinary haven where the flavors of Kauai are expertly crafted into each dish, and the breathtaking surroundings elevate the meal to a truly sensory celebration. Whether you are a seasoned traveler, a food enthusiast, or someone seeking a taste of authentic Hawaiian cuisine,

Oasis on the Beach beckons with open arms, inviting you to savor the essence of Kauai in every bite.

Red Salt

Red Salt is a culinary oasis situated at 2251 Poipu Road in Koloa, Hawaii. This restaurant, nestled within the Ko'a Kea Hotel & Resort, is a beacon of gastronomic delight on the southern shores of Kauai. With its commitment to blending Hawaiian flavors with global culinary techniques, Red Salt has earned a well-deserved reputation as one of the top dining establishments on the island.

The ambiance at Red Salt is both sophisticated and relaxed, offering patrons an inviting space to indulge in a memorable dining experience. The interior décor is a seamless fusion of modern elegance and tropical warmth, creating an atmosphere that is as visually pleasing as the dishes on the menu. Guests can choose between indoor seating or opt for an al fresco experience to bask in the balmy Hawaiian evenings.

What sets Red Salt apart is its dedication to using fresh, locally sourced ingredients. The culinary team, led by Executive Chef Noelani Planas, takes pride in curating a menu that reflects the vibrant and diverse culinary landscape of Kauai. The restaurant's commitment to sustainability is evident in its partnerships with local farmers and fishermen, ensuring a farm-to-table experience that is both ethical and delectable.

Now, let's delve into the heart of Red Salt – the menu. From appetizers to desserts, each dish is a carefully crafted masterpiece designed to tantalize the taste buds. One of the standout starters is the Red Salt Poke. This Hawaiian classic is elevated to new heights with the restaurant's signature touch, featuring impeccably fresh ahi tuna, soy ginger vinaigrette, and avocado mousse. The interplay of textures and flavors in this dish serves as a delicious prelude to the culinary journey that awaits.

Moving on to the main courses, the Kurobuta Pork Chop is a prime example of Red Salt's commitment to excellence. The succulent, locally sourced pork is paired with a flavorful sweet potato puree, apple chutney, and a bourbon demi-glace, creating a symphony of tastes that dance on the palate. For seafood enthusiasts, the Macadamia Nut-Crusted Mahi-Mahi is a must-try, showcasing the freshest catch from the surrounding waters.

Red Salt's commitment to providing a diverse menu is further exemplified in its vegetarian offerings. The Quinoa and Black Bean Burger, adorned with roasted red pepper aioli and avocado, is a flavorful option that caters to the discerning palate of vegetarian diners. This

attention to inclusivity ensures that Red Salt remains a dining destination for all tastes and preferences.

The dessert menu at Red Salt is a sweet finale to the culinary experience. The Lilikoi Crème Brulee is a popular choice, featuring the tropical flavors of passion fruit in a velvety custard with a perfectly caramelized sugar crust. Paired with a cup of locally sourced coffee or a dessert wine from the thoughtfully curated list, it provides a satisfying conclusion to the meal.

In addition to its regular menu, Red Salt frequently offers specials that showcase seasonal ingredients and innovative culinary techniques. This commitment to keeping the menu dynamic ensures that each visit to Red Salt is a unique experience, with the possibility of discovering new and exciting flavors with every return.

The beverage program at Red Salt is equally noteworthy. The expertly curated wine list features a selection of international and local wines, providing the perfect accompaniment to the diverse menu. The restaurant's skilled mixologists craft signature cocktails that reflect the spirit of the island, incorporating fresh tropical fruits and premium spirits to create libations that are both refreshing and sophisticated.

Service at Red Salt is as impeccable as the cuisine it serves. The attentive and knowledgeable staff enhances the overall dining experience, offering recommendations, ensuring dietary preferences are met, and creating an atmosphere of warmth and hospitality. The seamless coordination between the kitchen and the front-of-house team is a testament to the restaurant's commitment to providing a top-tier dining experience.

For those looking to celebrate a special occasion or host a private event, Red Salt offers private dining options. Whether it's an intimate dinner for two or a larger gathering, the restaurant's event coordinators work closely with guests to create a personalized and memorable experience.

Red Salt stands as a culinary gem on the shores of Kauai. With its dedication to showcasing the best of local ingredients, innovative culinary techniques, and a commitment to sustainability, it has rightfully earned its place as one of the island's premier dining establishments. Whether you're a visitor to Kauai or a local looking for an exceptional dining experience, Red Salt eckons with its tantalizing menu, inviting ambiance, and a commitment to culinary excellence hat is as bold and unforgettable as the island itself.

Postcards Café: A Culinary Haven in Hanalei

ostcards Café, nestled in the heart of Hanalei on the north shore of Kauai, stands as a culinary aven, beckoning locals and visitors alike with its charming ambiance and delectable cuisine. his establishment, housed in a plantation-era cottage, has become a culinary landmark, elebrated for its commitment to farm-to-table practices, sustainability, and a menu that ances with the flavors of the island.

ituated at 5-5075 Kuhio Highway, Postcards Café enjoys a prime location in Hanalei, offering atrons a view of the majestic mountains that frame the town. The plantation-era cottage xudes a rustic charm, inviting diners to step into a bygone era while enjoying a modern ulinary experience. The lush tropical surroundings and gentle Hawaiian breeze add to the verall enchantment of the setting.

he moment you enter Postcards Cafe, you are greeted by an atmosphere that seamlessly lends casual elegance with the laid-back charm of Hanalei. Wooden furnishings, vibrant local rtwork adorning the walls, and an abundance of natural light create a warm and welcoming pace. The open-air design allows patrons to dine in an alfresco setting, enhancing the overall ining experience with the sounds and scents of the island.

ostcards Café takes pride in its farm-to-table philosophy, emphasizing the use of fresh, locally ourced ingredients in every dish. The menu, a testament to the diverse bounty of Kauai, hanges daily based on the availability of seasonal produce and the catch of the day. This ommitment to sustainability not only supports local farmers and fishermen but also ensures hat diners experience the true essence of Kauai's culinary landscape.

he Menu

At the heart of Postcards Café's allure is its menu, a carefully curated selection of dishes that showcase the culinary prowess of the island. From appetizers to desserts, each item on the menu tells a story of flavor, creativity, and a deep connection to the local community.

Appetizers:

Begin your culinary journey with appetizers that tantalize the taste buds. The Ahi Tartare, a celebration of fresh, local tuna, showcases the delicate balance of flavors with hints of soy, sesame, and avocado. The Coconut Shrimp, a nod to Kauai's coastal offerings, presents succulent shrimp enveloped in a crisp coconut crust, served with a tangy lilikoi dipping sauce.

Entrees:

The entrees at Postcards Café promise a symphony of flavors inspired by Hawaiian traditions and global influences. The Macadamia Nut-Crusted Mahi-Mahi, a perennial favorite, embodies the essence of the islands with its crunchy macadamia crust and a drizzle of lilikoi butter. For those seeking a land-based delight, the Grilled Filet Mignon, cooked to perfection, is paired with a red wine reduction, creating a dish that delights carnivores and connoisseurs alike.

Desserts:

No culinary journey is complete without a sweet finale, and Postcards Café's dessert offerings are nothing short of divine. The Lilikoi Crème Brulee, a tropical twist on a classic, boasts a velvety custard infused with the bright and tangy flavors of passion fruit. The Chocolate-Haupi Torte, a marriage of rich chocolate and creamy coconut, is a decadent indulgence that leaves a lasting impression.

Complementing the exquisite menu is a thoughtfully curated beverage selection. The wine list features both local and international varietals, providing the perfect pairing for each dish. Creative and refreshing cocktails crafted from tropical fruits and spirits add a touch of island flair to the dining experience.

Beyond its culinary excellence, Postcards Café actively engages with the local community. By supporting local farmers, fishermen, and artisans, the restaurant contributes to the sustainability and growth of Kauai's vibrant food culture. This commitment to community is woven into the fabric of the establishment, creating a sense of shared responsibility and pride ostcards Café stands as a culinary gem in the tapestry of Kauai's dining scene. With its farm-to-able ethos, commitment to sustainability, and a menu that captures the essence of the island, his restaurant offers not just a meal but a gastronomic journey. Whether you're a discerning ood enthusiast or a casual diner seeking an authentic taste of Kauai, Postcards Café invites you o savor the flavors of the island in a setting that celebrates the rich tapestry of Hawaiian ulture. In every bite and every detail, Postcards Café tells a story—a story of Kauai, its people, nd the vibrant culinary legacy that continues to unfold in this enchanting corner of the Pacific.

O2 Natural Cuisine

lestled in the heart of Kapaa, Kauai, JO2 Natural Cuisine stands as a testament to the island's ommitment to natural and sustainable dining. This culinary haven, located at 4-971 Kuhio Hwy, wites diners on a journey that transcends the boundaries of conventional cuisine, offering a iverse menu that caters to a wide array of tastes and preferences.

s you step into JO2 Natural Cuisine, you're immediately enveloped in a warm and inviting tmosphere. The restaurant's décor combines modern elegance with a touch of island charm, reating a space that feels both sophisticated and comfortable. Natural elements such as wood nd stone are seamlessly integrated, providing a backdrop that complements the restaurant's ommitment to natural and locally sourced ingredients.

Vhat sets JO2 Natural Cuisine apart is its unwavering dedication to natural, organic, and ustainable dining. The culinary team, led by Executive Chef Jean-Marie Josselin, embraces the oncept of farm-to-table, ensuring that every dish reflects the freshest and finest ingredients hat Kauai has to offer.

he menu at JO2 Natural Cuisine is a celebration of flavors, textures, and culinary creativity. Vhether you're a seafood enthusiast, a vegetarian, or a meat lover, there's a dish to tantalize our taste buds. Start your culinary journey with the Lobster & Kauai Shrimp Ravioli, a dish that mbodies the essence of the island's bountiful seafood offerings. The delicate pasta envelopes ucculent pieces of lobster and shrimp, creating a harmonious blend of textures and flavors.

or those seeking a hearty and comforting option, the Braised Short Rib is a standout choice. low-cooked to perfection, the meat falls off the bone, delivering a melt-in-your-mouth xperience. Accompanied by locally sourced vegetables and a rich demi-glace, this dish is a estament to JO2's commitment to both taste and sustainability.

egetarians need not feel left out, as JO2 Natural Cuisine has curated a selection of plant-based lelights. The Grilled Vegetable Tower is a colorful medley of seasonal vegetables, showcasing the chef's skill in elevating simple ingredients to culinary art. Each bite bursts with the natural flavors of the vegetables, enhanced by the subtle notes of the accompanying herb-infused olive oil.

Beyond its delectable offerings, JO2 Natural Cuisine takes pride in its sustainability initiatives. The restaurant collaborates with local farmers and fishermen, ensuring a direct and responsible sourcing of ingredients. This commitment not only supports the local community but also contributes to the overall eco-conscious dining experience that JO2 strives to provide.

At the helm of JO2 Natural Cuisine is the esteemed Executive Chef Jean-Marie Josselin. With a culinary career spanning decades and a passion for innovative and sustainable cuisine, Chef Josselin brings a wealth of expertise to the table. His vision for JO2 is reflected not only in the menu but also in the overall dining experience, where every detail is thoughtfully curated to enhance the guest's journey.

JO2 Natural Cuisine isn't just a place to eat; it's an experience. The attentive and knowledgeable staff adds to the overall ambiance, providing insights into the menu and ensuring that each guest feels welcomed. The open kitchen design allows diners to witness the culinary magic as it unfolds, creating a sense of transparency and connection between the kitchen and the dining area.

No culinary journey is complete without a sweet conclusion, and JO2 Natural Cuisine delivers on this front as well. The dessert menu features indulgent creations such as the Lilikoi Cheesecake, a tropical twist on a classic favorite. The delicate balance of sweet and tangy flavors encapsulates the essence of Kauai's vibrant culinary scene.

Pair your meal with a selection from the thoughtfully curated wine list or explore the restaurant's signature cocktails. The libations complement the menu, offering a diverse range of options to suit every palate.

JO2 Natural Cuisine welcomes guests for dinner, creating an intimate and relaxed setting perfect for romantic evenings or celebratory gatherings. Reservations are recommended, especially during peak dining hours, ensuring that you secure a seat for your culinary adventure.

In the realm of Kauai's culinary landscape, JO2 Natural Cuisine stands as a beacon of natural and sustainable dining. From the carefully curated menu to the warm and welcoming ambiance, every aspect of the restaurant reflects a commitment to providing guests with a dining experience that goes beyond the ordinary.

As you savor each bite at JO2 Natural Cuisine, you not only indulge in exquisite flavors but also contribute to a movement that values the earth's bounty and treasures the connections forged hrough shared meals. It's not just a restaurant; it's a culinary sanctuary where passion, ustainability, and creativity converge to create a truly memorable dining experience.

Vhether you're a seasoned food enthusiast or a traveler eager to explore Kauai's culinary reasures, JO2 Natural Cuisine beckons you to embark on a gastronomic journey that celebrates he beauty of natural and locally sourced ingredients, one exceptional dish at a time.

Kauai Grill

auai Grill, situated at 5520 Ka Haku Rd in the breathtaking St. Regis Princeville Resort, stands s a culinary masterpiece on the lush island of Kauai. With an unmatched reputation, this estaurant is the brainchild of the acclaimed chef Jean-Georges Vongerichten, offering an nparalleled dining experience that seamlessly blends world-class cuisine with the stunning atural beauty of Hanalei Bay.

Jpon entering Kauai Grill, guests are immediately enveloped in an ambiance that is both ophisticated and relaxed. The design reflects the natural elements of Kauai, with rich wood ccents, contemporary furnishings, and floor-to-ceiling windows that frame panoramic views of he Pacific Ocean and the surrounding mountains. The result is a setting that effortlessly omplements the culinary artistry that awaits patrons.

he menu at Kauai Grill Is a testament to Chef Jean-Georges' commitment to using the freshest, ocally sourced ingredients. The culinary team crafts a symphony of flavors, drawing inspiration rom Hawaiian traditions while infusing each dish with a global twist. From the moment the first ourse arrives, diners embark on a gastronomic journey that celebrates the island's bounty.

ignature dishes at Kauai Grill showcase the diversity of the menu. The Ahi Tuna Tartare, a lelightful starter, showcases the freshness of local seafood, complemented by vibrant citrus lotes and the subtle heat of jalapeño. Moving on to the main courses, the Miso-Maple Crusted Black Cod is a revelation, marrying the sweetness of maple with the umami depth of miso, reating a dish that lingers on the palate. For those seeking a carnivorous delight, the Grilled Hawaiian Kampachi, adorned with a yuzu vinaigrette, is a harmonious blend of textures and lavors.

A visit to Kauai Grill is not merely a meal; it's a sensory experience. The open kitchen concept llows guests to witness the culinary magic as it unfolds, with skilled chefs meticulously preparing each dish. The attentive and knowledgeable staff adds to the overall ambiance, ensuring that every aspect of the dining experience is nothing short of exceptional.

The beverage program at Kauai Grill is as meticulously curated as its menu. The wine list boast an impressive selection of international and local labels, expertly chosen to complement the diverse flavors presented in each dish. The cocktail menu, featuring handcrafted creations inspired by the island's tropical essence, provides the perfect prelude to a memorable meal.

As night falls, Kauai Grill transforms into an intimate haven illuminated by soft lighting, creatin an atmosphere that is both romantic and refined. The outdoor terrace beckons diners to savor their meal against the backdrop of a Hawaiian sunset, casting a warm glow over the landscape

The commitment to sustainability is evident in every aspect of Kauai Grill's operations. The restaurant sources ingredients locally whenever possible, supporting the island's farmers and producers. This dedication to responsible dining aligns seamlessly with Kauai's ethos of preserving its natural beauty and cultural heritage.

Reviews from diners consistently applaud not only the culinary artistry but also the impeccable service and attention to detail. The seamless fusion of exquisite flavors, an inviting ambiance, and unparalleled views positions Kauai Grill as a culinary gem, not just on the island but in the wider culinary landscape.

In conclusion, Kauai Grill stands as a testament to the harmonious marriage of culinary innovation and natural beauty. Chef Jean-Georges Vongerichten's vision has manifested into a dining experience that transcends the ordinary, inviting patrons to indulge in the best of both worlds — the culinary delights of a world-renowned chef and the breathtaking allure of Kauai' landscapes. A visit to Kauai Grill is not just a meal; it's a celebration of flavors, a symphony of senses, and an immersion into the heart of culinary excellence on the Garden Isle.

Food Trucks and Street Food in Kauai

Kauai, known for its breathtaking landscapes and vibrant culture, is also a haven for food enthusiasts seeking unique and flavorful experiences. One of the best ways to explore the loca culinary scene is by indulging in the diverse offerings from food trucks and street vendors scattered across the island. Here's a glimpse into the delectable world of Kauai's street food:

1. *Da Crack – Tacos and Burritos*

Location: 2827 Poipu Road, Koloa

Da Crack is a hidden gem offering mouthwatering tacos and burritos. With a laid-back atmosphere, it's a favorite among locals and tourists alike. Try their fish tacos for a taste of Kauai's fresh seafood.

2. Puka Dog – Hawaiian-Style Hot Dogs

Location: 2360 Kiahuna Plantation Drive, Koloa

Puka Dog is a must-visit for hot dog enthusiasts. The unique blend of Hawaiian flavors, including their signature taro bun and tropical relishes, sets them apart. It's a delightful and satisfying quick bite.

3. Kauai Juice Co. – Fresh and Healthy Juices

Location: 4270 Kilauea Road, Kilauea

For a refreshing and healthy option, head to Kauai Juice Co. They specialize in cold-pressed juices made from locally sourced fruits and vegetables. Perfect for a quick pick-me-up while exploring the island.

4. Wishing Well Shave Ice – Shave Ice Delights

Location: 5-5080 Kuhio Highway, Hanalei

No trip to Kauai is complete without indulging in shave ice, and Wishing Well Shave Ice is a standout. With an array of flavors and toppings, it's a delightful treat to beat the island heat.

5. Hanalei Taro & Juice Co. – Taro-Based Creations

Location: 5-5161 Kuhio Highway, Hanalei

Dive into the local staple, taro, at Hanalei Taro & Juice Co. From taro smoothies to poi bowls, this food truck celebrates traditional Hawaiian ingredients with a modern twist.

6. Trucking Delicious – Gourmet Island Cuisine

Location: Varies; check their social media for updates

Trucking Delicious is a mobile culinary experience that moves around the island. With a menu that changes regularly, it's a great option for those looking to savor gourmet island cuisine prepared with fresh, local ingredients.

7. Kalapaki Beach Hut – Beachside Bites

Location: 3474 Rice Street, Lihue

Enjoy the laid-back vibes of Kalapaki Beach Hut, offering a variety of beachside bites. From fish tacos to loco moco, this food truck provides a taste of Kauai's diverse culinary scene.

SECTION 6: SHOPPING

Discovering Kauai's Local Markets

Kauai, known as the "Garden Isle," is not only renowned for its stunning natural beauty but also for its vibrant local markets. These markets offer a unique glimpse into the island's culture, providing an array of fresh produce, handmade crafts, and a taste of the local way of life. In this guide, we'll explore some of the must-visit local markets in Kauai along with their addresses, ensuring that your journey through these marketplaces is both enjoyable and seamless.

1. **Kauai Community Market**

Address: 3-1901 Kaumualii Hwy, Lihue, HI 96766

The Kauai Community Market, located in Lihue, is a lively gathering of local farmers, artisans, and musicians. Open on Saturdays, it offers a diverse range of fresh produce, including tropical fruits, vegetables, and unique island specialties. Visitors can also indulge in handmade crafts, jewelry, and traditional Hawaiian snacks. The live music and friendly atmosphere make it a perfect way to spend a Saturday morning immersing yourself in the local Kauai community.

2. **Hanalei Farmers Market**

Address: 5-5363 Kuhio Hwy, Hanalei, HI 96714

Nestled on the North Shore of Kauai, the Hanalei Farmers Market is a gem surrounded by lush landscapes. Operating on Saturdays, this market showcases the best of the region's agricultural bounty. From organic fruits to locally grown coffee, visitors can experience the flavors of Kauai in one place. Don't miss the chance to interact with farmers and artisans, gaining insight into the island's agricultural practices and the tight-knit community of Hanalei.

3. Koloa Sunshine Market

Address: 3461 Weliweli Rd, Koloa, HI 96756

For those exploring the southern part of Kauai, the Koloa Sunshine Market is a delightful stop. Open on Mondays, this market boasts an array of fresh fruits, vegetables, and flowers. The aroma of tropical blossoms fills the air as you wander through stalls brimming with pineapples, papayas, and exotic orchids. Engage with local vendors, learning about their farming techniques and the significance of agriculture in sustaining Kauai's unique ecosystem.

4. Kapaa Town Farmers Market

Address: 4-796 Kuhio Hwy, Kapaa, HI 96746

The Kapaa Town Farmers Market, held on Wednesdays, is a bustling market that perfectly encapsulates the island's spirit. With a mix of local produce, prepared foods, and handmade crafts, this market is a sensory delight. Stroll through the colorful stalls, tasting freshly prepared coconut treats or picking up souvenirs crafted by Kauai's skilled artisans. The market's central location in Kapaa makes it easily accessible for both residents and visitors exploring the eastern side of the island.

5. Waimea Town Market

Address: 9691 Kaumualii Hwy, Waimea, HI 96796

Situated in the historic town of Waimea on the west side of Kauai, the Waimea Town Market offers a unique blend of local flavors and cultural experiences. Open on Saturdays, it features fresh produce, handmade crafts, and a selection of ready-to-eat local delicacies. As you explore the market, take in the views of Waimea Canyon, often referred to as the "Grand Canyon of the Pacific," providing a stunning backdrop to your market adventure.

xploring Kauai's local markets is not just a shopping experience; it's a journey into the heart of he island's culture. Each market is a testament to the community's dedication to preserving nd sharing its traditions. Whether you're seeking fresh, tropical fruits or looking to connect /ith local artisans, Kauai's markets are a feast for the senses, offering a genuine taste of the sland's vibrant way of life. Plan your visits wisely, savor the local flavors, and immerse yourself n the rich tapestry of Kauai's markets.

Souvenirs

auai, the lush and captivating island in the Hawaiian archipelago, is not only a haven for atural beauty but also a treasure trove of unique souvenirs that encapsulate the spirit and ulture of this enchanting destination. As you explore the various corners of the island, you'll iscover an array of handcrafted items and keepsakes that make for perfect mementos of your auai adventure.

)ne of the most iconic and sought-after souvenirs from Kauai is the traditional Hawaiian lei. hese beautiful flower garlands, made with fragrant local blooms like plumeria and orchids, are ot only a symbol of hospitality but also a vibrant reminder of the island's tropical allure. 'isitors can find leis in various colors and styles, each carrying its own significance and charm.

or those with a penchant for art and craftsmanship, Kauai offers an abundance of locally made andcrafted items. From intricately carved koa wood products to vibrant quilts showcasing raditional Hawaiian patterns, the island's artisanal scene is rich and diverse. Consider bringing ome a piece of Kauai's artistic heritage with a wooden bowl, a meticulously woven lauhala hat, r a unique piece of pottery from one of the island's talented artisans.

auai's commitment to sustainability is evident in many of its souvenirs. Eco-friendly options uch as reusable bamboo utensils, organic skincare products, and recycled material accessories eflect the island's dedication to preserving its natural beauty. These thoughtful souvenirs not nly make for meaningful gifts but also contribute to the sustainable ethos that Kauai mbraces.

he island's connection to the ocean is beautifully represented in its marine-inspired souvenirs.)elicate seashell jewelry, intricately designed mother-of-pearl items, and hand-blown glass rnaments resembling ocean waves are just a few examples of the treasures you can find. 'hese souvenirs not only capture the essence of Kauai's coastal landscapes but also serve as eminders of the island's deep-rooted maritime culture.

No trip to Kauai is complete without savoring the delectable flavors of the island, and fortunately, these culinary delights can be taken home in the form of edible souvenirs. Indulge in the rich taste of Kauai-grown coffee, sample local honey infused with the island's diverse flora, or choose from an array of tropical jams and exotic spices. These gastronomic delights allow you to bring the distinct flavors of Kauai directly to your kitchen.

As you traverse the island, you'll encounter a myriad of shops and markets, each offering its own selection of Kauai souvenirs. The bustling towns of Hanalei, Kapa'a, and Poipu are particularly known for their charming boutiques and artisanal shops. Here, you can immerse yourself in the island's shopping scene, exploring the diverse array of souvenirs that reflect both Kauai's history and its contemporary cultural tapestry.

For those seeking a tangible connection to Kauai's natural wonders, consider a souvenir that incorporates elements of the island's flora and fauna. Dried plumeria blossoms, seashell-adorned accessories, or botanical prints celebrating the island's endemic plants are all thoughtful choices. These items not only serve as reminders of the island's biodiversity but also carry with them the energy of Kauai's natural landscapes.

For a truly personalized memento, many shops on the island offer customization services. Whether it's engraving your name on a piece of jewelry, personalizing a surfboard, or creating custom fragrance using local scents, these bespoke souvenirs allow you to take home a piece of Kauai that is uniquely yours.

The souvenirs of Kauai are as diverse and captivating as the island itself. Whether you're drawn to traditional crafts, sustainable products, or edible delights, there's a treasure waiting for every visitor. These souvenirs not only serve as tokens of your time on the Garden Isle but also embody the spirit of aloha that defines Kauai, making them enduring reminders of a truly unforgettable experience.

Unique Finds

Exploring Kauai is not just about its breathtaking landscapes and popular tourist spots; it's also about discovering the hidden gems that make this Hawaiian island truly unique. From quaint local markets to tucked-away boutiques, Kauai offers a treasure trove of distinctive finds that capture the essence of the island's culture, history, and creativity.

One of the first things that captivates visitors is the vibrant array of handmade crafts and artworks that reflect the rich tapestry of Kauai's artistic community. Local artisans often showcase their talents in small galleries and roadside stands, offering visitors a chance to take home a piece of the island's creative spirit. Whether it's a hand-carved wooden sculpture or a meticulously crafted piece of jewelry, these unique finds serve as tangible reminders of the island's commitment to preserving and celebrating its artistic heritage.

As you wander through Kauai's local markets, you'll encounter a delightful array of culinary treasures. The island's food scene is a fusion of traditional Hawaiian flavors and innovative culinary techniques. Local farmers and producers take pride in offering unique products that showcase the diversity of Kauai's agriculture. From exotic tropical fruits and honey to artisanal chocolates and coffee, these edible treasures provide a delicious way to savor the distinct tastes of the island.

For those seeking a more immersive cultural experience, Kauai's historical sites and museums offer a glimpse into the island's fascinating past. Unearth the stories of ancient Hawaiians at archaeological sites or delve into the island's plantation era history at sugar museums. These unique finds provide a deeper understanding of Kauai's cultural roots and the forces that have shaped its identity over the centuries.

Nature enthusiasts will find their own set of unique discoveries on Kauai. The island is home to an incredible diversity of flora and fauna, some of which can only be found in this specific corner of the world. Botanical gardens showcase the island's stunning array of tropical plants, and bird watchers can delight in spotting native species in their natural habitats. These encounters with Kauai's unique ecosystems offer a chance to connect with the island's natural beauty on a profound level.

As you explore Kauai's shopping scene, you'll encounter a variety of boutique stores offering curated selections of clothing, accessories, and home décor. Many of these items draw inspiration from the island's laid-back lifestyle, incorporating tropical motifs and vibrant colors. Whether you're in search of a stylish souvenir or a fashionable piece to add to your wardrobe, these boutique finds reflect the casual elegance that defines Kauai's sense of style.

Venture off the beaten path, and you may stumble upon hidden gems that showcase the island's commitment to sustainability and community. Farmers' markets, for instance, not only provide fresh, locally grown produce but also serve as gathering places for residents and visitors alike. These markets are not just about shopping; they're about connecting with the community, learning about local initiatives, and participating in the island's commitment to sustainable living.

In the realm of unique finds, Kauai extends beyond tangible objects and into the realm of experiences. Engaging with the local community through events, festivals, and cultural activities reveals the heart and soul of the island. Whether it's a traditional Hawaiian hula performance, community festival celebrating local arts, or a gathering to honor ancient traditions, these experiences offer a window into the vibrant and welcoming spirit of Kauai.

Kauai's unique finds go far beyond the typical tourist fare. They encompass the island's artistic expressions, culinary delights, historical narratives, natural wonders, and the intangible but powerful sense of community. Exploring these unique finds not only adds depth to your visit but also allows you to take a piece of Kauai's distinctive charm home with you, creating lasting memories of a truly special place in the heart of the Pacific.

SECTION 7: CULTURE AND HISTORY

Native Hawaiian Culture

Native Hawaiian culture is a rich tapestry woven from the threads of history, tradition, and a profound connection to the land and sea. Rooted in a deep reverence for nature, the indigenous people of Hawaii, known as Kanaka Maoli or Native Hawaiians, have cultivated a unique way of life that reflects their deep spiritual connection to the islands.

At the core of Native Hawaiian culture is the concept of 'aina,' meaning land. The land is not merely a physical entity; it is a living, breathing ancestor that sustains and nurtures the people. Hawaiians believe in the reciprocal relationship between humans and the land, emphasizing the importance of stewardship and respect for the natural world.

Language plays a pivotal role in preserving and transmitting Native Hawaiian culture. The Hawaiian language, once on the brink of extinction, has experienced a revitalization in recent years. Efforts to teach the language in schools and communities have contributed to a resurgence of cultural pride. The language is a vessel for the oral traditions, chants, and stories passed down through generations, encapsulating the wisdom and knowledge of the ancestors.

The hula, a traditional dance form, is another cornerstone of Native Hawaiian culture. Far more than a mere performance, the hula is a sacred art that encapsulates stories, genealogy, and spiritual connection. Each movement, gesture, and expression within the dance conveys a deeper narrative, bridging the past with the present.

eremonial practices, such as the 'kapu' system, once governed every aspect of Hawaiian life. These societal regulations dictated behavior, land use, and resource management. Although the kapu system was abolished in the early 19th century, its influence endures in the cultural consciousness, leaving an indelible mark on the way Hawaiians approach their relationship with each other and the land.

The importance of family, or 'ohana,' is paramount in Native Hawaiian culture. Ohana extends beyond blood relations to include close friends and those who share a sense of community. The concept reinforces the interconnectedness of individuals and emphasizes collective responsibility.

Traditional voyaging and navigation, exemplified by the ancient art of wayfinding, underscore the resourcefulness and ingenuity of Native Hawaiians. Navigators relied on the stars, wind, and ocean currents to traverse the vast Pacific, connecting the islands and expanding the Hawaiian worldview.

The spiritual practices of Native Hawaiians are deeply ingrained in daily life. The connection to ancestral deities, or 'akua,' is evident in rituals, ceremonies, and the acknowledgment of sacred sites. These practices foster a sense of unity and harmony with the natural and supernatural realms.

Artistry and craftsmanship are woven into the fabric of Native Hawaiian culture. From intricate kapa (bark cloth) making to the creation of finely carved tools and implements, Hawaiians have long exhibited a keen appreciation for aesthetic expression. Today, contemporary Native Hawaiian artists continue to draw inspiration from traditional forms while pushing the boundaries of artistic innovation.

Native Hawaiian culture is a living, breathing entity that thrives in the hearts and minds of the people. It is a celebration of the interconnectedness of all things, a dance between past and present, and a testament to the enduring spirit of a people deeply rooted in the land and sea that sustain them.

Historical Sites in Kauai: Exploring the Rich Past of the Garden Isle

The island is home to several historical sites that offer a glimpse into its cultural heritage. From ancient Hawaiian temples to missionary settlements, each site tells a unique story of Kauai's past.

Waioli Mission House and Church

Location: 5-6601 Kuhio Hwy, Hanalei, HI 96714

Nestled in the heart of Hanalei, the Waioli Mission House and Church provide a fascinating insight into the early missionary history of Kauai. Built in the mid-19th century, these structures showcase the architectural and cultural influences of that time.

The mission house, constructed in 1836, served as the residence for early Christian missionaries. Visitors can explore the well-preserved rooms and artifacts, gaining an

understanding of the challenges faced by the missionaries and the impact of their work on the local community. The adjacent Waioli Church, built in 1912, is a beautiful example of Hawaiian architecture.

Maha'ulepu Heritage Trail

Location: Shipwreck Beach to Punahoa Point

For those seeking a journey through both history and nature, the Maha'ulepu Heritage Trail offers a scenic coastal hike along Kauai's southern shore. This trail takes you through ancient Hawaiian archaeological sites, including petroglyphs and house platforms.

The petroglyphs, etched into lava rock, provide a direct connection to Kauai's indigenous people and their artistic expressions. As you walk along the trail, you'll also encounter the remains of heiau (temples) and ancient fishing villages, painting a vivid picture of the island's past.

Kilauea Lighthouse

Location: 3580 Kilauea Rd, Kilauea, HI 96754

Perched on the northernmost point of Kauai, the Kilauea Lighthouse stands as a historic beacon with panoramic views of the Pacific Ocean. Built in 1913, the lighthouse guided ships through the treacherous Kauai waters for decades.

Today, the lighthouse and its surrounding area are a designated wildlife refuge, home to a variety of seabirds. Visitors can explore the lighthouse and the adjacent keeper's dwelling, gaining insight into the challenges faced by early lighthouse keepers.

Grove Farm Homestead

Location: 4050 Nawiliwili Rd, Lihue, HI 96766

The Grove Farm Homestead offers a journey back in time to the days of sugar plantations in Hawaii. Dating back to the mid-19th century, this site was once a bustling sugar plantation and the residence of George N. Wilcox, a prominent figure in Kauai's history.

The homestead includes the original plantation house, servants' quarters, and various outbuildings. Guided tours provide visitors with a comprehensive understanding of the island's plantation era, its impact on the local community, and the evolution of Kauai over the years.

These historical sites in Kauai not only showcase the island's past but also contribute to the preservation of its cultural heritage. Exploring these locations provides a deeper appreciation for the diverse history that has shaped the Garden Isle into the unique destination it is today.

Museums and Exhibits

Museums and exhibits on Kauai offer visitors an opportunity to delve into the island's past, exploring its traditions, art, and history. Here's a comprehensive guide to some of the noteworthy museums and exhibits on the island, complete with addresses for your convenience.

1. *Kauai Museum*

Address: 4428 Rice St, Lihue, HI 96766

Immerse yourself in the island's history at the Kauai Museum. With exhibits ranging from ancient Polynesian voyaging to the plantation era, the museum provides a captivating journey through time. Discover artifacts, photographs, and interactive displays that showcase the diverse cultural tapestry of Kauai.

2. *Grove Farm Homestead Museum*

Address: 4050 Nawiliwili Rd, Lihue, HI 96766

Step into the past at the Grove Farm Homestead Museum, a living history site that offers a glimpse into the island's sugar plantation era. The museum includes historic buildings, a railway, and guides in period costumes, providing a fascinating experience of Kauai's agricultural heritage.

3. Waioli Mission House

Address: 5-6601 Kuhio Hwy, Hanalei, HI 96714

Nestled in the charming town of Hanalei, the Waioli Mission House showcases missionary life i the 19th century. Explore the well-preserved house, gardens, and artifacts, gaining insights into the impact of missionaries on Kauai's culture and community.

4. West Kauai Technology & Visitor Center

Address: 9565 Kaumuali î Hwy, Waimea, HI 96796

Uncover the technological advancements and history of West Kauai at the Technology & Visito Center. The exhibits highlight the region's agricultural and industrial past, with a focus on innovation and sustainability.

5. Hawaiian Music Hall of Fame

Address: Kilohana Plantation, 3-2087 Kaumualii Hwy, Lihue, HI 96766

Located at the historic Kilohana Plantation, the Hawaiian Music Hall of Fame celebrates the ric musical heritage of the islands. Interactive exhibits and memorabilia pay homage to legendary musicians, offering visitors a melodic journey through Hawaii's cultural evolution.

6. Art House 429

Address: 4290 Kuhio Hwy, Princeville, HI 96722

For a contemporary twist, visit Art House 429 in Princeville. This gallery features local artists, showcasing a vibrant collection of paintings, sculptures, and crafts. It's an excellent opportunit to appreciate the modern artistic expressions emerging from Kauai.

7. Kokee Natural History Museum

Address: Kokee State Park, Mile Marker 15, Kekaha, HI 96752

Dive into the ecological wonders of Kauai at the Kokee Natural History Museum. Located in the pristine Kokee State Park, this museum provides valuable insights into the island's unique flora and fauna through interactive exhibits and educational programs.

8. Limahuli Garden & Preserve

Address: 5-8291 Kuhio Hwy, Hanalei, HI 96714

While primarily a botanical garden, Limahuli offers educational exhibits on Hawaiian plant conservation. Learn about the importance of preserving native species and the role of traditional Hawaiian ahupua'a land management.

9. Princeville Center – Historical Room

Address: 5-4280 Kuhio Hwy, Princeville, HI 96722

The Historical Room at Princeville Center provides a curated collection of photographs, artifacts, and documents that trace the development of Princeville and the surrounding areas. It's a small but insightful stop for those interested in the local history of this community.

10. Kauai Coffee Estate

Address: 870 Halewili Rd, Kalaheo, HI 96741

Explore the history and art of coffee production at the Kauai Coffee Estate. The museum on the estate educates visitors on the journey from bean to cup, highlighting the significance of coffee in Kauai's agricultural landscape.

Whether you're interested in history, art, or the natural environment, Kauai's museums and exhibits offer a diverse range of experiences that contribute to a deeper understanding of the island's unique identity. Take the time to explore these cultural gems as you immerse yourself in the beauty and heritage of Kauai.

Annual Events in Kauai: A Year-Round Celebration

1. Kauai Film Festival

Address: Kauai Community College Performing Arts Center, 3-1901 Kaumualii Hwy, Lihue, HI 96766

Every January, cinephiles gather on the Garden Isle for the Kauai Film Festival. Featuring a diverse selection of films, workshops, and Q&A sessions with filmmakers, this event is a celebration of cinematic art in the heart of the Pacific.

2. Waimea Town Celebration

Address: Various locations in Waimea town

The Waimea Town Celebration, held annually in February, is a week-long event celebrating Kauai's unique history and culture. From traditional Hawaiian music and dance to local cuisine and historical reenactments, this festival offers a vibrant immersion into the island's heritage.

3. Kauai Chocolate & Coffee Festival

Address: Historic Hanapepe Town, 3970 Hanapepe Rd, Hanapepe, HI 96716

Indulge your taste buds at the Kauai Chocolate & Coffee Festival, an annual event in Hanapepe that takes place every April. Attendees can sample locally grown coffee, exquisite chocolates, and learn about the island's thriving agricultural scene.

4. Kauai Polynesian Festival

Address: Kapaa Beach Park, 4460 Nehe Rd, Kapaa, HI 96746

Embrace the spirit of aloha at the Kauai Polynesian Festival, a lively event held in June at Kapaa Beach Park. Enjoy traditional Polynesian dance, music, and cuisine, creating a rich cultural experience for locals and visitors alike.

5. Koloa Plantation Days

Address: Various locations in Koloa

July marks the Koloa Plantation Days, a festival commemorating the island's sugar plantation heritage. Attendees can engage in historical tours, parades, and cultural demonstrations throughout Koloa, providing insight into Kauai's economic history.

6. Kauai Mokihana Festival

Address: Various locations in Lihue

Celebrating Hawaiian music and culture, the Kauai Mokihana Festival, held in September, features concerts, hula performances, and workshops. Join in the festivities to experience the island's musical traditions in the heart of Lihue.

7. Kauai Marathon

Address: Grand Hyatt Kauai Resort & Spa, 1571 Poipu Rd, Koloa, HI 96756

Lace up your running shoes for the Kauai Marathon, an annual event in September that takes participants through the scenic landscapes of Poipu. Whether you're a seasoned runner or a spectator, this event promotes health and wellness against the backdrop of Kauai's stunning vistas.

8. Kauai Pow Wow

Address: Kapaa Beach Park, 4460 Nehe Rd, Kapaa, HI 96746

In October, the Kauai Pow Wow invites locals and visitors to join in celebrating Native American and indigenous cultures. With traditional dance, arts, and crafts, this event fosters cross-cultural understanding and appreciation.

9. Kauai Festival of Lights

Address: Historic County Building, 4396 Rice St, Lihue, HI 96766

December brings the enchanting Kauai Festival of Lights. The Historic County Building in Lihue transforms into a festive wonderland, showcasing unique holiday displays and local artistry, making it a must-visit for those embracing the holiday spirit on the island.

These annual events in Kauai provide a wonderful opportunity to immerse yourself in the island's vibrant culture, history, and community spirit. Whether you're a culture enthusiast, a foodie, or someone seeking an active adventure, Kauai's diverse calendar of events has something for everyone.

Made in the USA
Columbia, SC
04 August 2024